THE ULTIMATE BEGINNER SERIES®

ACOUSTIC GUITAR

Revised Edition

Keith Wyatt

Alfred Music
P.O. Box 10003
Van Nuys, CA 91410-0003
alfred.com

ISBN-10: 0-7390-8196-9 (Book & CD)
ISBN-13: 978-0-7390-8196-9 (Book & CD)

ISBN-10: 0-7390-8203-5 (Book, CD & DVD)
ISBN-13: 978-0-7390-8203-4 (Book, CD & DVD)

ISBN-10: 0-7579-8165-8 (DVD)
ISBN-13: 978-0-7579-8165-4 (DVD)

Cover photographs:
Martin dreadnought courtesy of Martin Guitars.
Blue energy © iStockphoto.com / Raycat

Contents

Track 1
INTRO SONG

Track 2
TUNING NOTES

Section One: The Basics

PARTS OF THE GUITAR

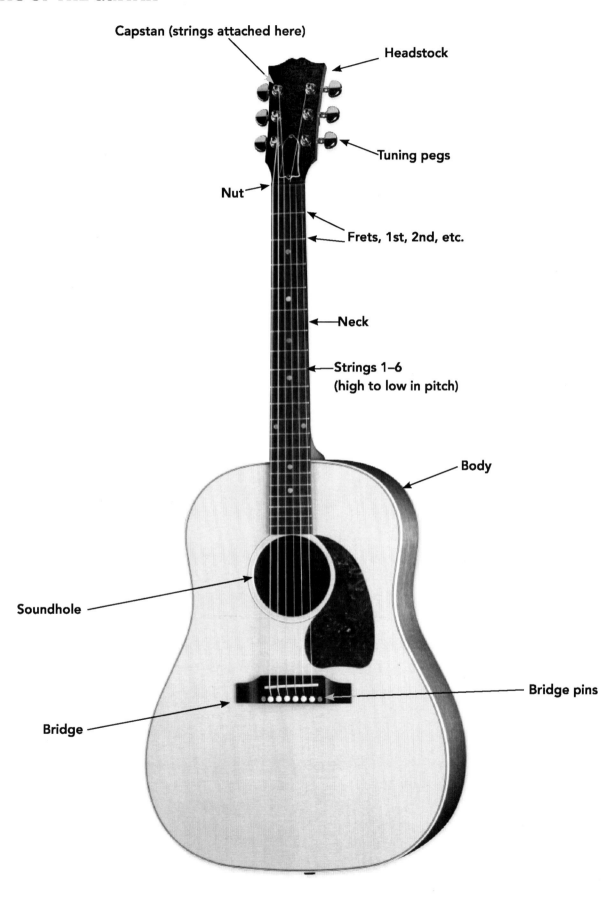

Capstan (strings attached here)

Headstock

Tuning pegs

Nut

Frets, 1st, 2nd, etc.

Neck

Strings 1–6
(high to low in pitch)

Body

Soundhole

Bridge pins

Bridge

THE THREE BASIC GUITAR TYPES Track 3

THE NYLON-STRING ACOUSTIC (CLASSIC GUITAR)

The nylon-string acoustic guitar has a nice mellow tone and has several advantages for beginners. The strings are much easier to press to the fretboard so they don't cut into your fingers the way steel strings do. Also, the neck is wider than on a typical steel-string guitar, which makes fingering chords a little easier. The classic guitar is perfectly suited to intimate, unaccompanied guitar performances.

THE ELECTRIC GUITAR

The electric guitar has come to dominate popular music. It is an extremely versatile instrument capable of producing everything from mellow jazz tones and biting funk riffs to the screaming, over-the-top, dizzying pyrotechnics of rock's reigning guitar virtuosos.

The Steel-String Acoustic

The steel-string acoustic guitar is perhaps the most versatile and common
guitar type. Although it is a little bit harder to play than the nylon string
guitar, the steel-string acoustic has a loud, bright, ringing tone that
clearly projects to the listener. This guitar is excellent for backing a singer.

STRINGS

Strings are available in three basic gauges: light, medium and heavy. I suggest you
begin with light or medium gauge strings.

PICKS

Picks come in many shapes, sizes and thicknesses. For acoustic guitar, I recommend
light to medium thickness. For electric, the thicker picks seem to work best. Experiment
to find the size and shape you are most comfortable with.

TUNING METHODS Track 4

Tuning to a Keyboard

The six strings of a guitar can be tuned to a keyboard by matching the sound of each open guitar string to the keyboard notes as indicated in the diagram.

Note: You will hear the intonation better, and your guitar will stay in better tune, if you loosen the strings and tune them *up* to pitch rather than starting above the correct pitch and tuning down.

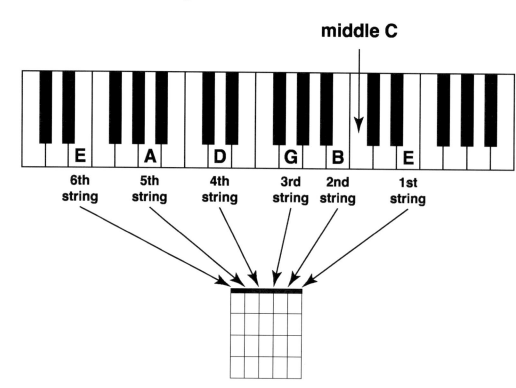

Electronic Tuners

Many brands of small, battery-operated tuners are available. These are excellent for keeping your guitar in perfect tune and for developing your ear to hear intonation very accurately. Simply follow the instructions supplied with the electronic tuner.

Tuning the Guitar to Itself—The "Fifth Fret" Method

1. Either assume your 6th string "E" is in tune, or tune it to a piano or some other fixed pitch instrument.

2. Depress the 6th string at the 5th fret. Play it and you will hear the note "A," which is the same as the 5th string played open. Turn the 5th string tuning peg until the pitch of the open 5th string ("A") matches that of the 6th string/5th fret (also "A").

3. Depress the 5th string at the 5th fret. Play it and you will hear the note "D," which is the same as the 4th string played open. Turn the 4th string tuning peg until the pitch of the open 4th string ("D") matches that of the 5th string/5th fret (also "D").

4. Depress the 4th string at the 5th fret. Play it and you will hear the note "G," which is the same as the 3rd string played open. Turn the 3rd string tuning peg until the pitch of the open 3rd string ("G") matches that of the 4th string/5th fret (also "G").

5. Depress the 3rd string at the 4th fret (not the 5th fret as in the other strings). Play it and you will hear the note "B," which is the same as the 2nd string played open. Turn the 2nd string tuning peg until the pitch of the open 2nd string ("B") matches that of the 3rd string/4th fret (also "B").

6. Depress the 2nd string at the 5th fret. Play it and you will hear the note "E," which is the same as the 1st string played open. Turn the 1st string tuning peg until the pitch of the open 1st string ("E") matches that of the 2nd string/5th fret (also "E").

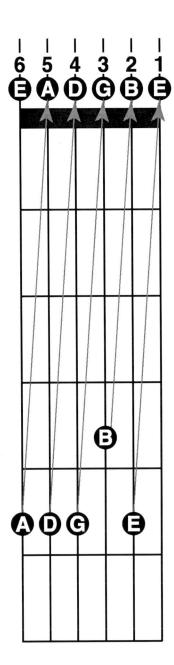

CHANGING STEEL-STRING ACOUSTIC STRINGS*

Eventually, whether because a string has broken on its own, or because through repeated use it is no longer "tunable," you will have to change your strings. Be prepared! Always keep the following in your guitar case:

1. A set of extra strings.
2. A pair of wire cutters.
3. A string winder.

(All three of these items are available at your local music store.)

CHANGING STRINGS

1. First, remove the bridge pin to release the ball end from the bridge. Unwrap the other end of the string from around the tuning peg.

2. Insert the ball end of the new string into the hole in the bridge and replace the bridge pin.

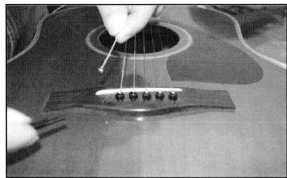

3. Once the string has been inserted into the bridge, feed the other end through the hole in the tuning peg, making sure to leave some slack in the string.

4. Bend the end slightly and, with your string winder, begin to tighten the string.

5. Trim the excess string off with your wire cutters.

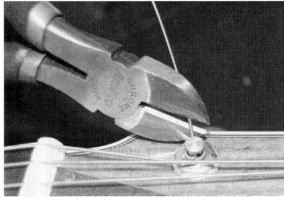

* For information on changing electric or classic guitar strings, see *I Just Bought My First Guitar* (00-22705).

READING RHYTHM NOTATION

At the beginning of every song is a time signature. $\frac{4}{4}$ is the most common time signature:

$$\frac{4}{4}$$ = FOUR COUNTS TO A MEASURE
= A QUARTER NOTE RECEIVES ONE COUNT

The top number tells you how many counts per measure.
The bottom number tells you which kind of note receives one count.

The time value of a note is determined by three things:

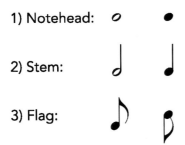

1) Notehead:

2) Stem:

3) Flag:

This is a whole note. The notehead is open and has no stem. In $\frac{4}{4}$ time, a whole note receives 4 counts.

This is a half note. It has an open notehead and a stem. A half note receives two counts.

This is a quarter note. It has a solid notehead and a stem. A quarter note receives one count.

This is an eighth note. It has a solid notehead and a stem with a flag attached. An eighth note receives one half count.

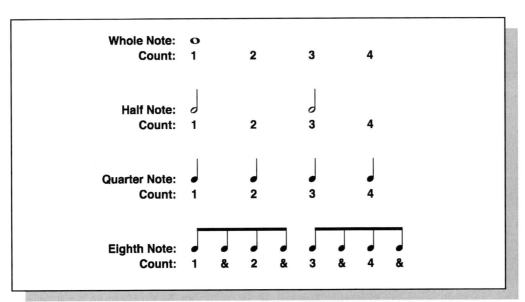

Rests indicate silence and there is a rest that corresponds to each note value. A whole rest ▬ lasts four beats, a half rest ▬ lasts two beats, a quarter rest ⅃ lasts one beat, and an eighth note rest ⅋ lasts one half count.

READING STANDARD MUSIC NOTATION

Music is written on a *staff*. The staff consists of five lines and four spaces between the lines:

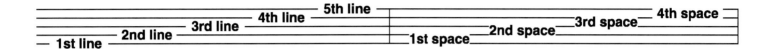

The names of the notes are the same as the first seven letters of the alphabet: A B C D E F G. The notes are written in alphabetical order. The first (lowest) line is "E":

Notes can extend above and below the staff. When they do, *ledger lines* are added. Here is the approximate range of the guitar from the lowest note, open 6th string "E," to a "B" on the 1st string at the 17th fret.

The staff is divided into *measures* by *bar lines*. A heavy double bar line marks the end of the music.

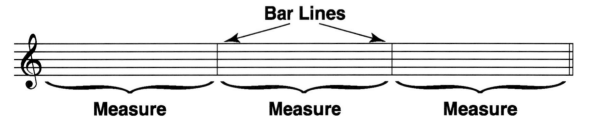

READING TABLATURE (TAB) AND FRETBOARD DIAGRAMS

Tablature (TAB) illustrates the location of notes on the neck of the guitar. This illustration compares the six strings of a guitar to the six lines of tablature.

Notes are indicated by placing fret numbers on the strings. An "0" indicates an open string.

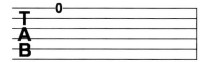

This tablature indicates to play the open, 1st and 3rd frets on the 1st string.

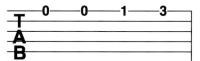

Tablature is usually used in conjunction with standard music notation. The rhythms and note names are indicated by the standard notation and the location of those notes on the guitar neck is indicated by the tablature.

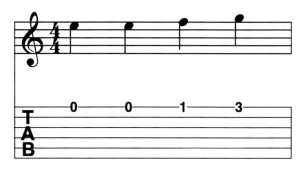

Chords are often indicated in *chord block diagrams.* The vertical lines represent the strings and the horizontal lines represent the frets. Scales are often indicated with guitar *fretboard diagrams.* Here the strings are horizontal and the frets are vertical.

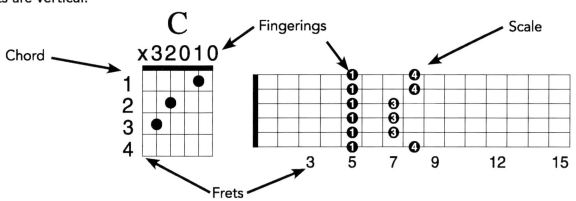

Section Two: Open-Position Chords

THE SIX BASIC OPEN-POSITION CHORDS

These are the most fundamental chords to all styles of guitar playing. "Open"-position chords contain open strings, which ring out loud and clear. The sound of a ringing open chord is probably the most identifiable guitar sound there is. Whether you play acoustic or electric guitar, these six chords will be some of the main chords you will use throughout your lifetime.

E MAJOR   Track 5

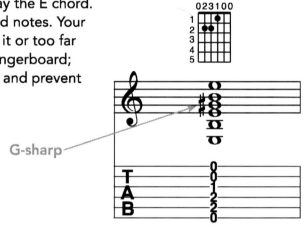

The dots indicate which notes to play with your finger, the zeros indicate open strings and "x" indicates a string that should not be played. Play the E chord. Make sure you get a clear sound without any buzzing or muffled notes. Your fingertips should be placed just behind the fret—not on top of it or too far behind it. Also, the fingertips should be perpendicular to the fingerboard; if they lean at an angle they will interfere with the other strings and prevent them from ringing.

> ♯ = *Sharp.* A sharp sign indicates the note is played one fret higher than its *natural* position.

G-sharp

A MAJOR 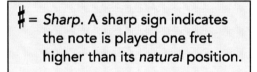 Track 6

Alternate Fingering

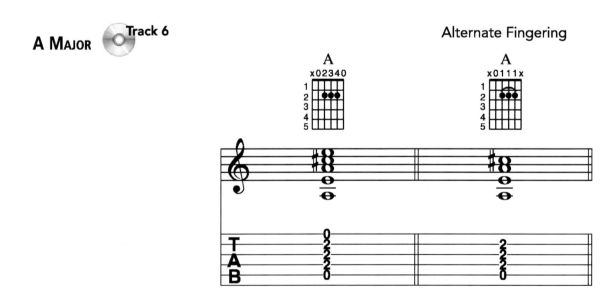

Notice that in the alternate fingering there is no 1st-string "E." This is OK; it's still an A chord.

D Major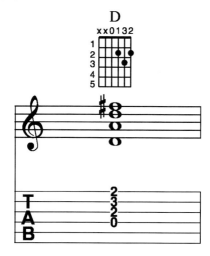

Track 7

The D chord uses just the top four strings. Play the chord making sure you can get a good clear, ringing tone.

STRUMMING

Relax your left hand and strum with a constant down-up motion from your wrist. Strike the strings evenly with both the down-strum and, as your hand returns to playing position, with the up-strum. Down-strums are indicated with this symbol: ◻. Up-strums are indicated with this symbol: V.

Listen to the recording and when you're ready, play along.

EXAMPLE 1: FIRST STRUMMING PATTERN
Track 8

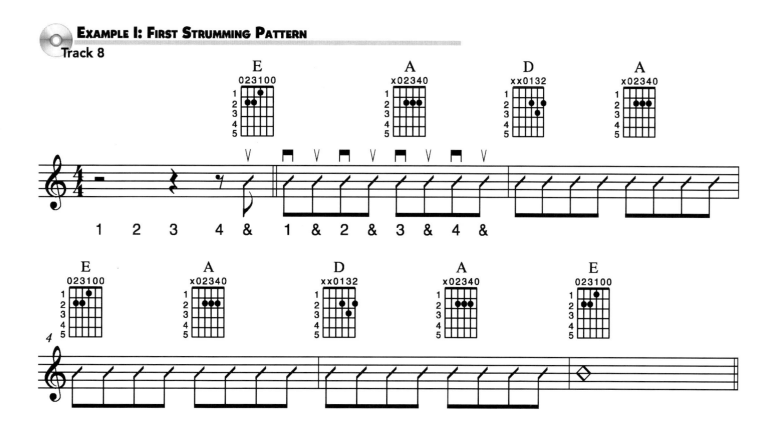

Track 9

G MAJOR

Tip: In order to play this chord cleanly, it is essential that you play on your fingertips, holding your fingers perpendicular to the neck. Keeping your left-hand thumb down in the center of the neck will help keep your fingers in the best position to avoid interfering with the other strings.

EXAMPLE 2

Track 10

Now try combining the G chord with the D chord. Notice both chords use the same three fingers:

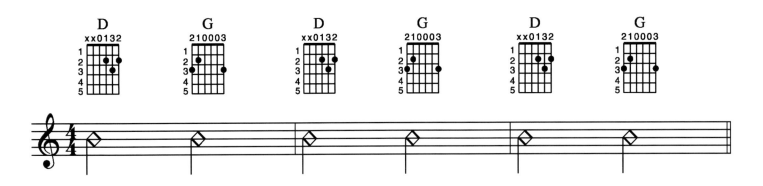

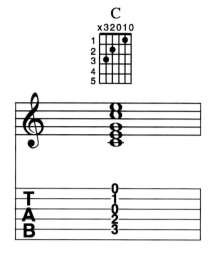

C Major

Track 11

Remember: Hold your fingers perpendicular to the neck making sure they touch only the strings they are playing and do not interfere with the other strings.

Example 3

Track 12

Practice moving back and forth between the C and G chords.

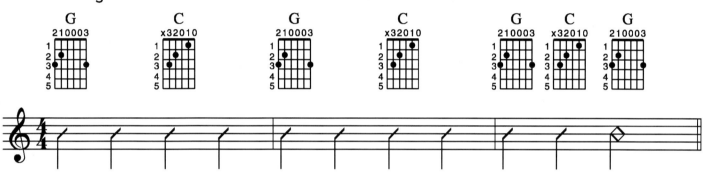

B7 Chord

Track 13

The G, D, C and E chords each contain three different notes. The B7 is a four-note chord ("B," "D♯," "F♯," "A").

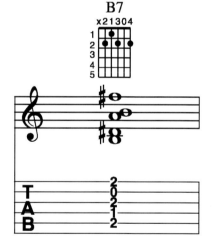

Example 4

Track 14

Now try this next example, which switches between the E and B7 chords.

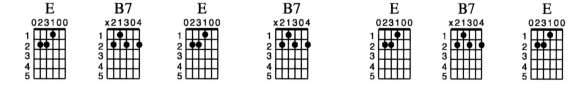

THE BLUES PROGRESSION (IN FOUR KEYS)

The blues progression is the most common chord progression. The typical blues progression is 12 measures long and uses the 1st, 4th and 5th chords of the key. To find the 1st, 4th and 5th chords (usually indicated with Roman numerals: I, IV and V), simply count up through the alphabet from the key note.

For Example:	Blues in the Key of "A":	A	B	C	D	E	F	G	A
		I			IV	V			
	Blues in the Key of "G":	G	A	B	C	D	E	F	G
		I			IV	V			
	Blues in the Key of "E":	E	F	G	A	B	C	D	E
		I			IV	V			
	Blues in the Key of "D":	D	E	F	G	A	B	C	D
		I			IV	V			

EXAMPLE 5: STRUM PATTERN A

Track 15.1

The next progression can be played with a variety of "strum" patterns. First try this simple "quarter-note" (one strum per beat) pattern. It can be played with either your pick, for a clear, bright sound; or your thumb, which gives it a darker, warmer sound. Listen to the recording to hear the difference.

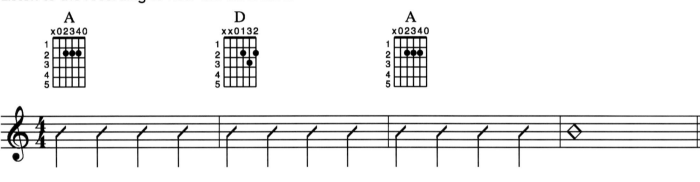

EXAMPLE 6: STRUM PATTERN B

Track 15.2

This next pattern uses both down- and up-strokes of the pick. Your right hand should maintain a constant down-up motion, hitting the strings on all of the down-strokes and on some of the up-strokes.

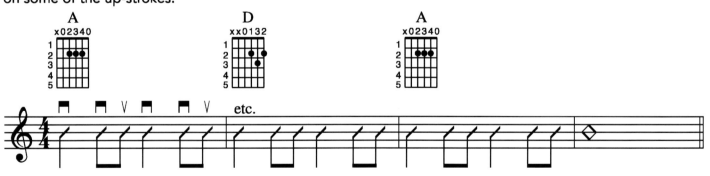

EXAMPLE 7

Track 16

The strumming example on the next page takes the blues progression through four keys: "A," "G," "E," and "D." It uses just the six chords you've learned so far: A, D, E, G, C and B7. Play along with the recording using the two rhythms you've just learned. When you're comfortable with the chord changes, try making up some rhythms of your own.

BLUES IN FOUR KEYS

//// = This kind of *slash notation* means to play any appropriate rhythm.

DOWN-UP STRUMMING

As you've already seen in Example 6, picking (or strumming) consists of two elements: the down-stroke and the up-stroke. Again, your right hand should maintain a constant down-up motion, striking the strings on not only the down-stroke, but also on some of the up-strokes.

EXAMPLE 8
Track 17

Here is a typical alternating strum pattern played over an E chord.

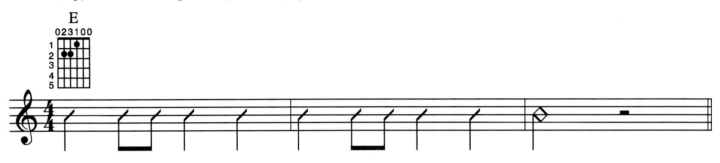

EXAMPLE 9
Track 18

Now let's apply the strum pattern from the previous example to the chord progression: E–D–A–E.

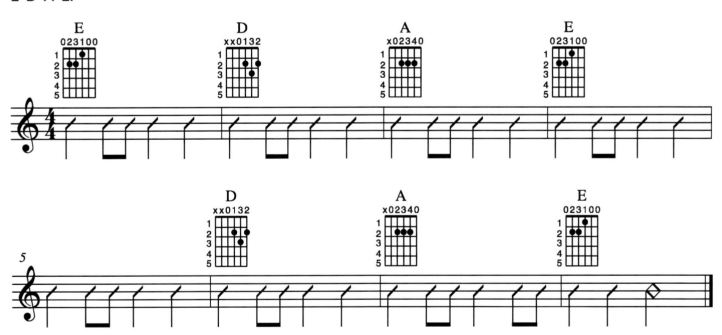

BASS/CHORD STRUM PATTERNS

One of the most common acoustic guitar strumming techniques is the bass/chord strumming pattern. First play the bass note (the root) of the chord, then strum the rest of the chord.

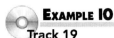

EXAMPLE 10
Track 19

Here is an example using an E chord. Play the lowest note ("E" on the 6th string) and then strum the higher strings. Use all down-strokes.

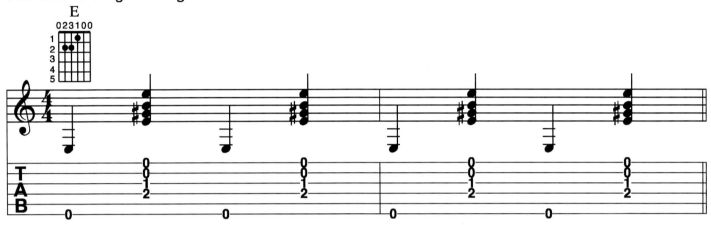

EXAMPLE 11
Track 20

Here is an example using an A chord. Play the lowest note ("A" on the 5th string) and then strum the higher strings. It's okay to look down at your picking hand if that helps.

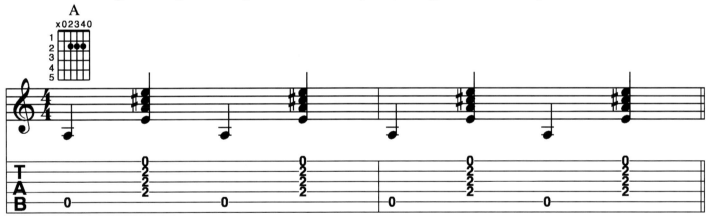

EXAMPLE 12
Track 21

Here is an example using a D chord. Play the lowest note ("D" on the 4th string) and then strum the higher strings.

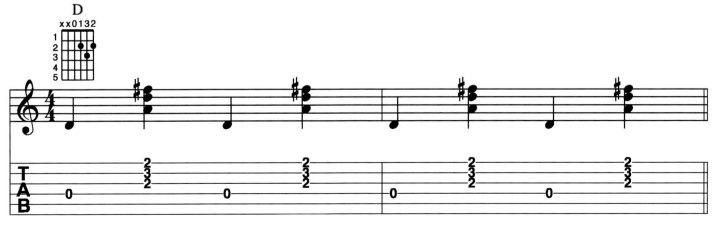

EXAMPLE 13
Track 22

Now try the bass/strum technique with the G chord. Again, play the lowest note (G on the 6th string) and then strum the higher strings.

EXAMPLE 14
Track 23

Now try the bass/strum technique on the C chord. The root is the 5th-string "C."

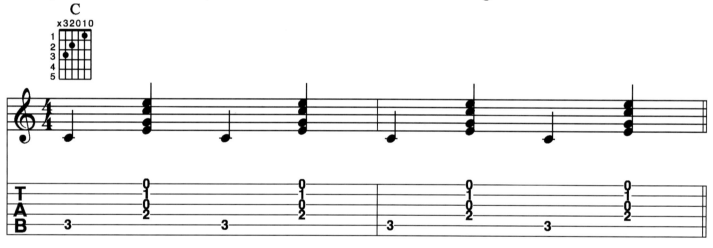

EXAMPLE 15
Track 24

Finally, let's try the bass/strum technique on the B7 chord. The root is the 5th-string "B."

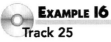

EXAMPLE 16

Track 25

Now put the bass/strum pattern in the context of a song using the chords G, C, and D. Practice the example until you can shift smoothly from one chord to the next without stopping or breaking up the rhythm.

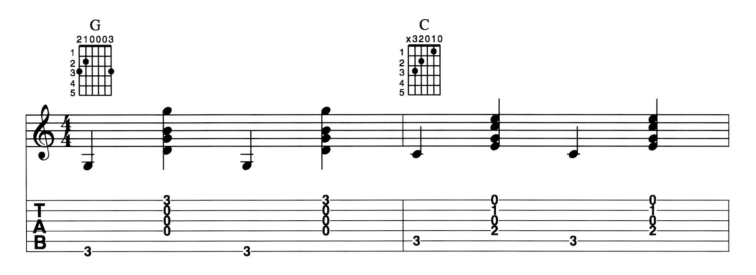

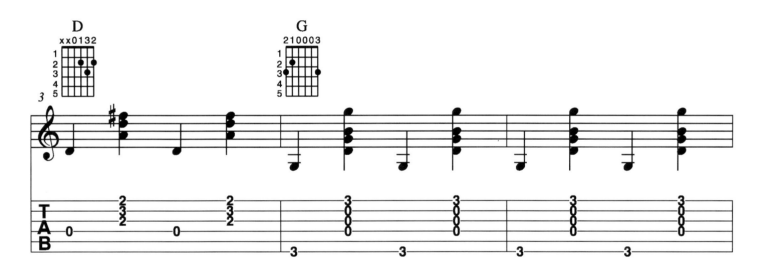

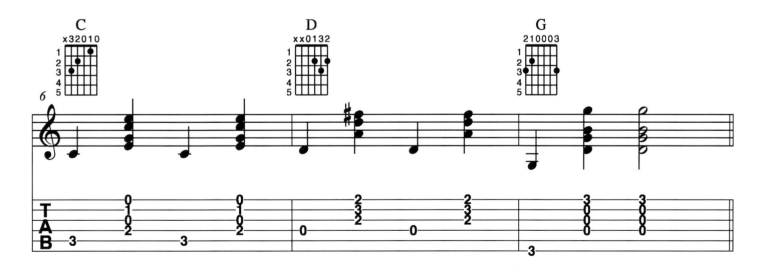

THE ALTERNATING BASS/STRUM PATTERN

The most common variation on the bass/strum pattern is to alternate between two different bass notes.

 **EXAMPLE 17**
Track 26

The simplest alternating bass pattern is to first play the lowest note, strum, then play the next highest bass note, then strum again. So for an E chord, the pattern would be: 6th string "E"–strum, 5th string "B"–strum. Again, use all down-strokes.

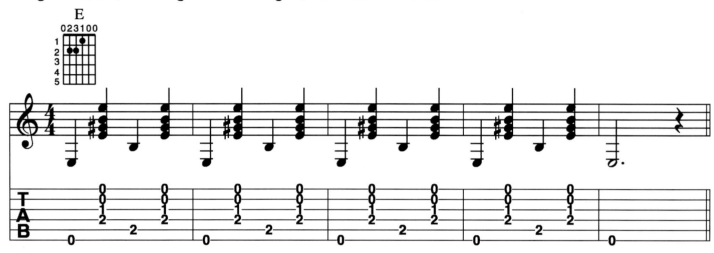

Note: Usually when playing alternating bass/chord patterns, it sounds best to "skip" or "miss" (omit) the bass notes when you strum the chord.

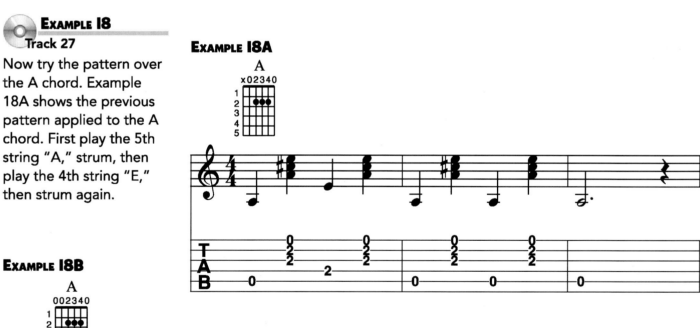

EXAMPLE 18
Track 27

Now try the pattern over the A chord. Example 18A shows the previous pattern applied to the A chord. First play the 5th string "A," strum, then play the 4th string "E," then strum again.

EXAMPLE 18A

EXAMPLE 18B

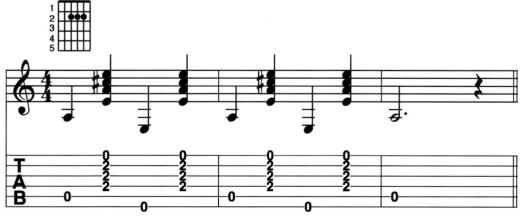

Example 18B shows a variation on the pattern: First play the 5th string "A," strum, now instead of playing the 4th string "E," play the low 6th string "E," then strum again. Again, use all down-strokes.

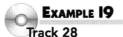 **EXAMPLE 19**
Track 28

EXAMPLE 19A

Now try the pattern over the D chord. Example 19A shows the basic pattern applied to the D chord. First play the 4th string "D," strum, then play the 3rd string "A," then strum again.

EXAMPLE 19B

Since the 3rd string "A" is a little too high to provide a good bass, try using the 5th string as the alternate bass instead: First play the 4th string "D," strum, now instead of playing the 3rd string "A," play the low 5th string "A," then strum again.

 EXAMPLE 20
Track 29

EXAMPLE 20A

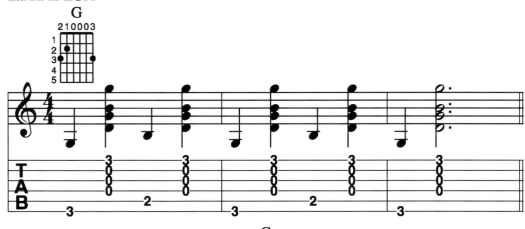

Now try the pattern over the G chord. Example 20A alternates between the 6th-string "G" and the 5th-string "B."

EXAMPLE 20B

Example 20B alternates between the 6th-string "G" and the 4th-string "D." (Again, notice how we often omit the note "D" on the strum.)

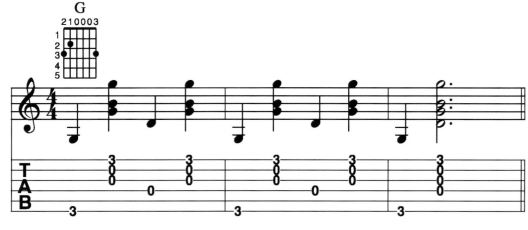

EXAMPLE 21
Track 30

For the C chord alternate between the 5th-string "C" and the 4th-string "E."

EXAMPLE 21A

EXAMPLE 21B
Example 21B shows a nice variation on the alternating bass pattern. Play the 5th-string "C," strum, then shift your 3rd finger from the "C" to the 6th-string "G," then strum again. Notice that we only strum the top four strings. This pattern will take a little practice, but soon you'll have it down.

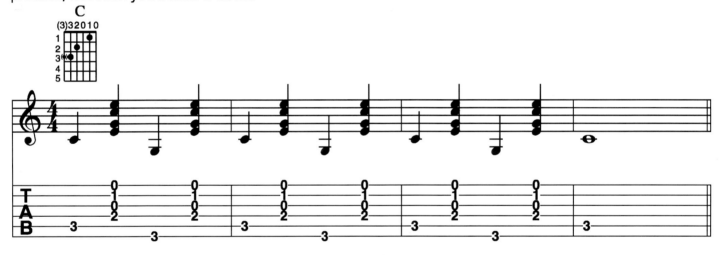

EXAMPLE 22
Track 31

EXAMPLE 22A
We can apply the same type of patterns to the B7 chord. First try alternating between the 5th-string "B" and the 4th-string "D♯."

EXAMPLE 22B

Example 22B uses the same type of finger shifting as you used with the C chord in Example 21B. Play the 5th string "B," strum, then shift your 2nd finger from the "B" to the 6th string "F♯," then strum again.

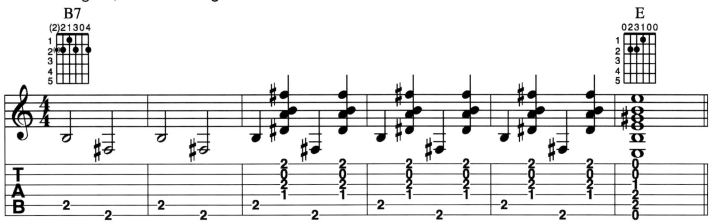

EXAMPLE 23
Track 32

This example combines all the chords you've learned with the alternating bass pattern.

CHORD CATEGORIES

There are three categories of chords: Major, Minor, and Dominant. With these three types of chords, you can play basically any pop or rock song. You already know five basic open position major chords: E, D, C, A, and G.

Minor Chords: Minor chords differ from major chords by only one note: the 3rd. (To find the "3rd," count up three from the root, which is by definition the 1st note). By lowering the 3rd of any major chord one fret, the chord becomes a minor chord.

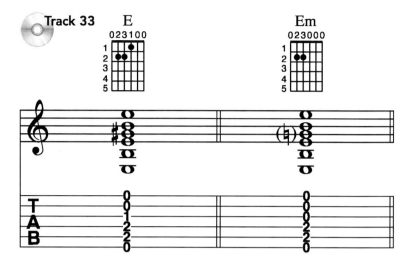

 **EXAMPLE 24**

Track 34

Play back and forth between the E and Em chords:

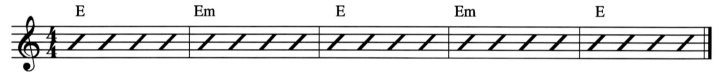

Notice again that the difference between the A and Am, and D and Dm chords is only one note (the 3rd).

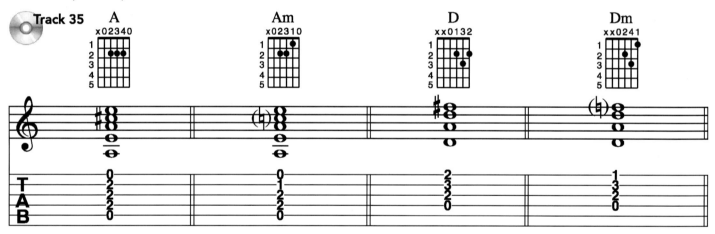

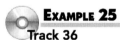 **EXAMPLE 25**

Track 36

Play back and forth between the A and Am chords:

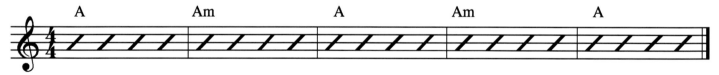

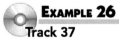 **EXAMPLE 26**

Track 37

Play back and forth between the D and Dm chords:

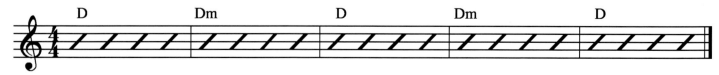

Dominant 7th Chords: Dominant chords differ from major chords by the addition of one note: the 7th. To find the "7th," count up seven in the alphabet (10 frets) from the root (1). Adding the 7th to a major chord makes it a dominant 7th chord.

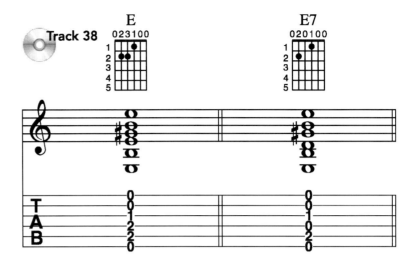

 EXAMPLE 27
Track 39

EXAMPLE 27A
Play back and forth between the E and E7 chords. Listen closely to the difference in sound the one new note makes:

EXAMPLE 27B
The difference between the A and A7, and D and D7 chords is again the addition of one note: the 7th.

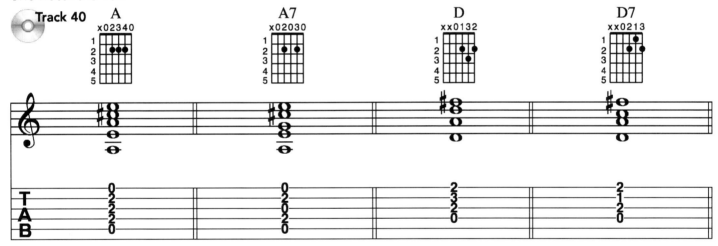

 EXAMPLE 28
Track 41

Play back and forth between the A and A7 chords:

 **EXAMPLE 29**
Track 42

Play back and forth between the D and D7 chords:

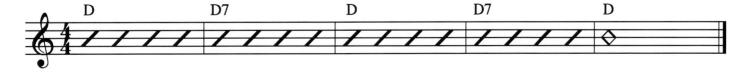

The open position G chord can be converted to a dominant chord as shown here. Try fingering the G chord with your 2nd, 3rd, and 4th fingers. This will make the change to G7 easier.

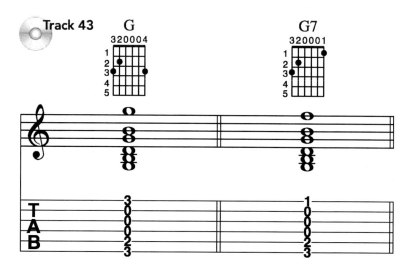

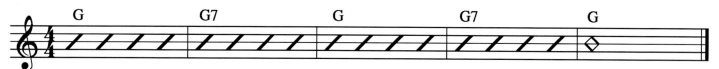

EXAMPLE 30
Track 44

Play back and forth between the G and G7 chords:

Now try converting the C to a C7. This is done by adding the 4th finger to the 3rd string.

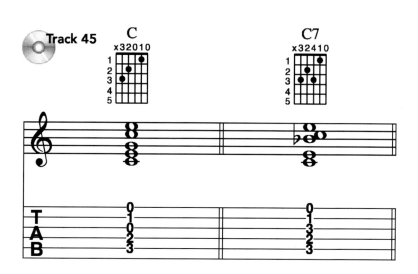

EXAMPLE 31
Track 46

Play back and forth between the C and C7 chords:

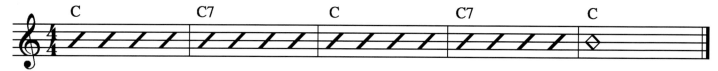

Section Three: Fingerpicking

So far, all the music in this book has been playable with either a pick or your thumb. Fingerpicking involves using the thumb and fingers independently of one another. This gives you the ability to play separate bass lines and melodies, all at the same time.

Example 32
Track 47

Hold an E chord. With the thumb of your picking hand, play an alternating bass from the 6th-string "E" to the 4th-string "E." Gently rest your index finger on the high "E" string while playing the steady quarter-note alternating bass with your thumb.

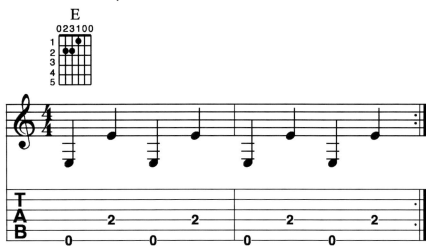

Example 33

Continue to hold the E chord while playing the alternating bass with your thumb. Play the high "E" string with an up-stroke of your index finger. The up-stroke of your index finger should happen at the same time as the down-stroke of your thumb. Notice that the bass notes (thumb) are written stems down and the melody notes (index finger) are written stems up.

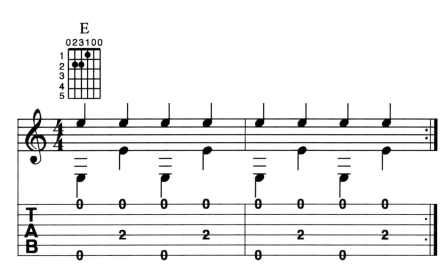

Example 34
Track 48

Now trying plucking the high "E" string with your index finger in between the thumb strokes. This is a little tricky at first. Keep playing this example until it feels easy and natural.

⌒ = *Tie.* A curved line that joins two or more notes of the same pitch that last the duration of the combined note values.

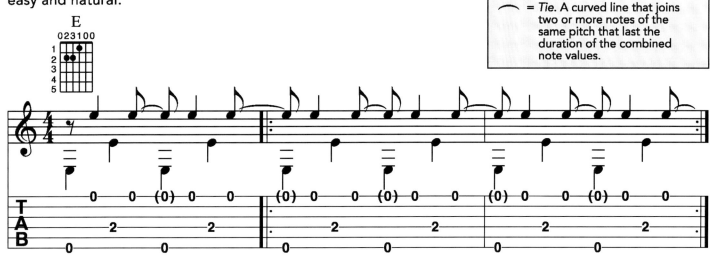

EXAMPLE 35
Track 49

The real beauty of this technique becomes apparent when you begin developing patterns that mix plucking on the beat (with the bass note) and plucking off the beat (in between the bass notes). Practice this example until the alternating thumb becomes automatic—as if it is functioning independently of your fingers.

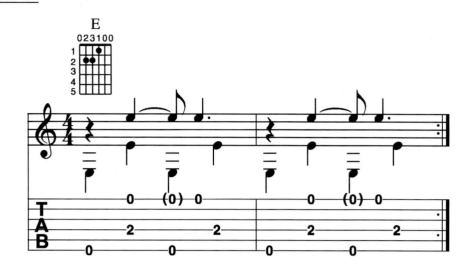

EXAMPLE 36
Track 50

Now try applying the same pattern to an A chord. Begin with just the alternating thumb, then add the index finger on the beat, then move the index finger in between the beats and finally play the complete pattern as in the previous example.

EXAMPLE 37
Track 51

Now apply the fingerpicking pattern to a G chord. As you begin to feel comfortable with these fingerpicking patterns, it would be a good idea to begin substituting your right-hand middle or ring fingers for your index finger on the top string. Eventually you will want to use all three fingers in varying combinations.

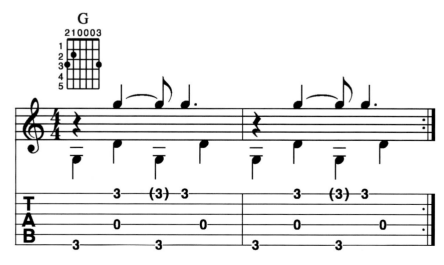

EXAMPLE 38

Track 52   In Example 19 we began using an alternate bass note for the D chord: the 5th-string "A" below the 4th-sting "D." In this fingerpicking example your thumb will alternate between the 4th-string "D" and both the 3rd- and 5th-string "A" notes. Practice just the thumb movement until it feels natural (Example 38A). Then add your index finger (Example 38B).

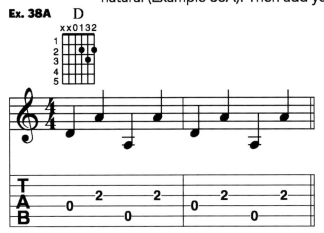

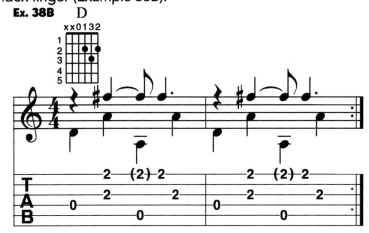

EXAMPLE 39

Track 53   For the C chord your thumb will alternate between the 5th-string "C," the 4th-string "E" and the 6th-string "G." As in Example 21B you will have to shift your 3rd finger back and forth from "C" to "G." Practice just the thumb movement until it feels natural (Example 39A). Then add your index finger (Example 39B).

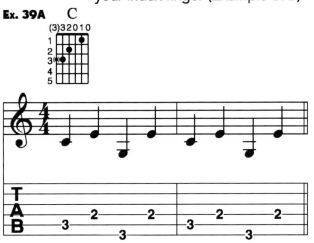

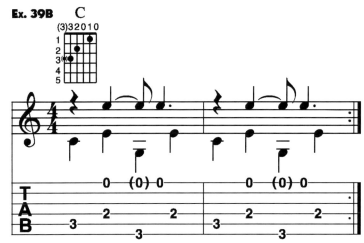

EXAMPLE 40

Track 54   Now apply the previous pattern to the B7 chord. You will have to shift your 2nd finger back and forth from the 5th to the 6th strings (see Example 22B). Again, practice just the thumb movement until it feels natural (Example 40A). Then add your index finger (Example 40B).

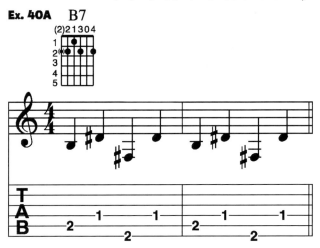

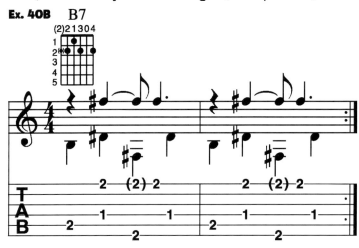

EXAMPLE 41

Track 55

This example combines the fingerpicking patterns with a complete chord progression.

Once the alternating thumb begins to feel "automatic," you'll be able to begin developing many variations on this pattern. Experiment with adding your middle and ring fingers in developing new patterns.

Section Four:
Hammer-Ons and Pull-Offs with Chords

One way to add new sounds and make your chords more interesting is to add and subtract certain notes from the chords as you play. We will use two different slurring techniques to add and subtract these notes:

1) A *hammer-on* is when you push (or "hammer") a left-hand finger onto a string with enough force to sound the note without using your picking hand.

2) A *pull-off* occurs when you release a left-hand finger from the string with a slight downward motion—actually plucking the string with the tip of your left-hand finger; again, sounding the note without using your picking hand.

EXAMPLE **42**
Track 56

We can add a note to the E chord by "hammering" the 4th finger down on the 3rd string. This changes the chord from an E major to an E suspended 4.

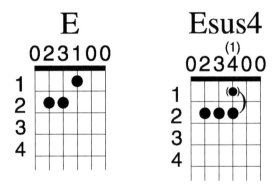

Play along with the recording. Then try making up some of your own patterns, switching between the E and Esus4 chords. Sometimes, sus4 chords are just called "sus" (for example, Esus instead of Esus4).

EXAMPLE **43**
Track 57

We can add other notes to the E chord. These diagrams indicate an added note on the 2nd string. This changes the chord from an E major to an E6. The next two diagrams show an added note on the 1st string. This alters the chord from an E major to an Eadd9. The notes are "added" using the hammer-on technique, and released using the pull-off technique.

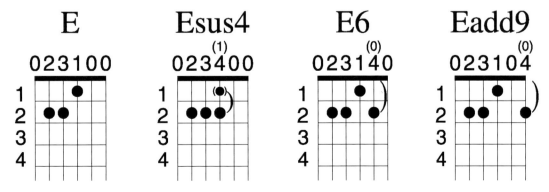

Again, play along with the recording. Then try making up some of your own patterns switching between the E/E6 and E/Eadd9 chords.

By moving your 4th finger up one fret you can add a "D" note to the A chord forming a Dsus. By lifting your 4th finger off the 2nd string you form an Asus2 chord.

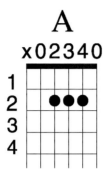
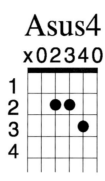
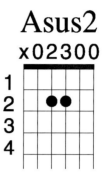

Again, play along with the recording. Then try making up some of your own patterns, switching between the A, Asus4, and Asus2 chords.

By "hammering" your 4th finger on the 1st string G you can change the D chord to Dsus, and by "pulling-off" your 2nd finger you can form Dsus2.

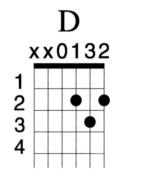
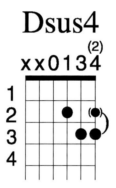
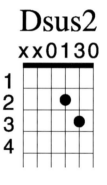

Again, play along with the recording. Then try making up some of your own patterns switching between the D, Dsus4, and Dsus2.

If you finger the G chord with your 2nd, 3rd, and 4th fingers your 1st finger will then be available for use on the 2nd string to form the Gsus4 chord.

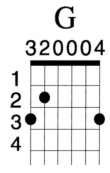
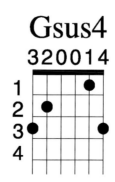

EXAMPLE 47

Track 61

For the C chord, the 4th finger can be hammered-on to the 4th string to form a Csus4 chord. The 3rd finger can be pulled-off the 4th string to form a Csus2.

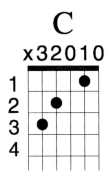
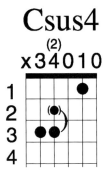
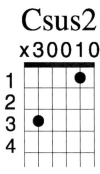

EXAMPLE 48

Track 62

Minor chords can be embellished in the same way as major chords by adding and subtracting notes, usually using the hammer-on and pull-off slurring techniques.

For A minor, adding the 4th finger on the 2nd string changes A minor to Asus4. Pulling-off the 1st finger forms an Asus2.

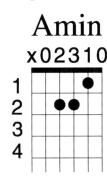
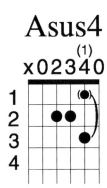
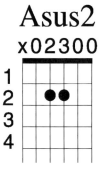

For D minor, adding the 4th finger on the 1st string changes D minor to Dsus4. Pulling-off the 1st finger forms a Dsus2.

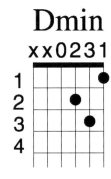
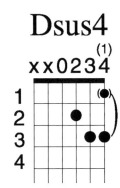
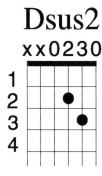

Again, play along with the recording. Then try making up some of your own patterns, switching between the various chords and their "colorations."

THE CAPO

So far, all of the chords you've learned have been first position "open-string" chord voicings. Using just these chords you are well on your way towards playing many popular songs in the keys of C, G, D, A, and E.

EXAMPLE 49
Track 63

With a capo you can transpose these chord fingerings to work in almost any key. For example, if you place the capo at the 3rd fret, all of the open string notes will be transposed up three frets. So if you then finger an E chord, it will sound as a G chord, and an A chord will sound as a C chord, etc.

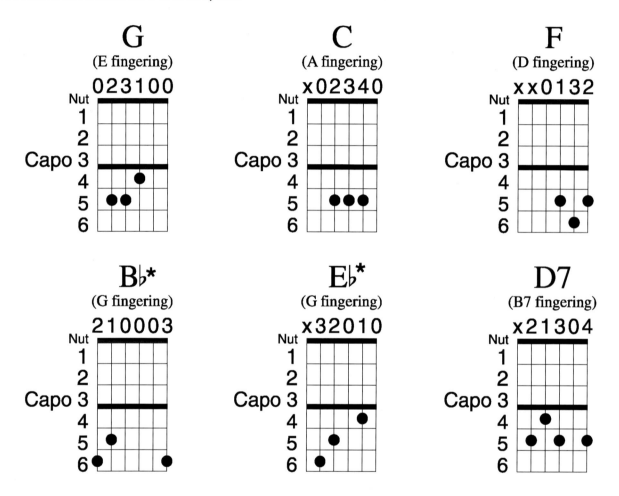

The capo is especially handy when you want to accompany a singer (or yourself). When the key of a song is too low, you can always bring it up higher by using the capo.

It is usually best to think of the song in the "fingering" key, locating the capo at whichever fret places the chords at a good pitch for the singer.

> ***** ♭ = *Flat.* A flat sign indicates the note is played one fret lower than its natural position.

Section Five: Barre Chords

There are two types of barre chords: those with their root on the 6th string and those with their root on the 5th string. Before we learn the barre chords let's first learn the notes on those two strings.

EXAMPLE 50
Track 64

This diagram shows the location of the natural (no sharps or flats) notes on the 6th string. It is useful to remember that there is a whole step (two frets) between all adjacent natural notes except for "E–F" and "B–C," which are separated by a half step (one fret).

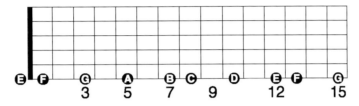

Here are the notes and tablature for the notes on the "E" string. Play these notes until you have them memorized.

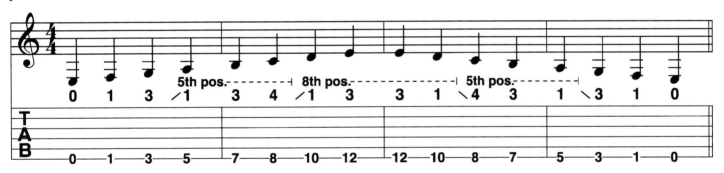

EXAMPLE 51
Track 65

This diagram shows the location of the natural (no sharps or flats) notes on the 5th string. Again, remember that there is a whole step (two frets) between all adjacent natural notes except for "E–F" and "B–C," which are separated by a half step (one fret).

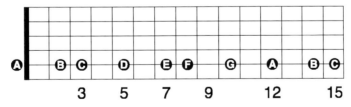

Here are the notes and tablature for the notes on the "A" string. Play these notes until they are memorized.

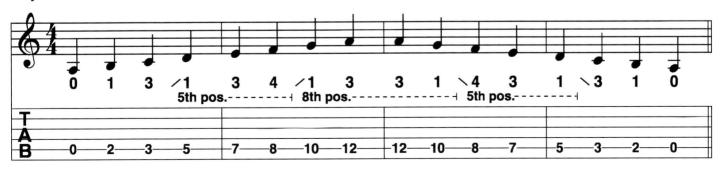

THE "E"-TYPE BARRE CHORD

So far we've only worked on open position chords. With barre chords you can leave the open position and play all around the neck.

Barre Chords: A barre chord is a chord in which two or more of the strings are played by one finger laying across those strings forming a "barre."

 EXAMPLE 52
Track 66

The most popular type of barre chord is based on the common E chord. To form the barre chord:

1) Re-finger the E chord with your 2nd, 3rd, and 4th fingers.

2) Shift your fingers up one fret.

3) Lay your 1st finger across all six strings at the 1st fret.

Practice each of the following chords, then try moving the barre chord to each fret on the neck and saying the name of the chord aloud.

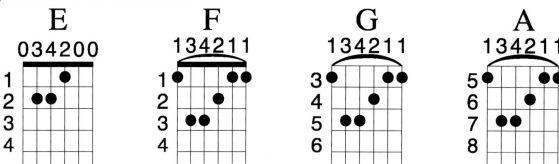

Tip: To add strength to your index finger barre, turn that finger slightly to the side so that the hard, outside edge of the finger forms the barre; not the soft, fleshy part on the inside.

 EXAMPLE 53
Track 67

Now convert the E minor to a barre chord. Again, practice each of these chords and then try playing them all over the neck, saying the name of the chord aloud.

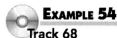 **EXAMPLE 54**
Track 68

Now convert the E7 to a barre chord. Again, practice each of these chords and then try playing them all over the neck, saying the name of the chord aloud.

THE "A"-TYPE BARRE CHORD

The next most popular type of barre chord is based on the common A chord. To form the "A" type barre chord:

1) Shift your 2nd, 3rd, and 4th fingers up one fret.

2) Lay your 1st finger across the top five strings at the 1st fret.

EXAMPLE 55

Track 68

Practice each of the following chords, then try moving the barre chord to each fret and saying the name of the chord aloud. Notice the optional fingering which requires a 3rd-finger barre across the middle strings. When using this optional fingering, you'll probably mute the 1st string with your 3rd finger. Practice both fingerings and see which works best for you.

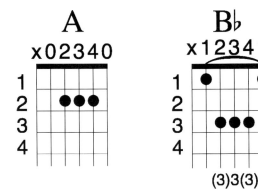
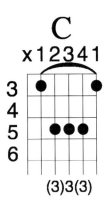
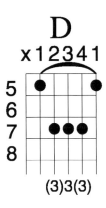

EXAMPLE 56

Track 69

Now convert the A minor to a barre chord. Again, practice each of these chords and then try playing them all over the neck, saying the name of the chord aloud.

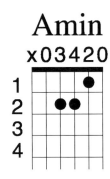
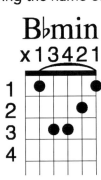
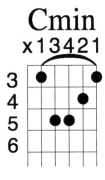
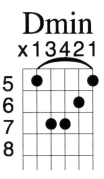

EXAMPLE 57

Now convert the A7 to a barre chord. Again, practice each of these chords and then try playing them all over the neck, saying the name of the chord aloud.

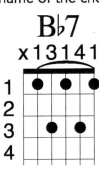
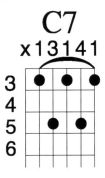

Chord Chart

OPEN-POSITION CHORDS

A
x02340
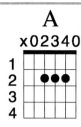

Amin
x02310
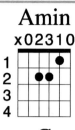

A7
x02030
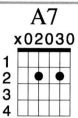

B7
x21304
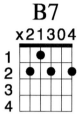

C
x32010
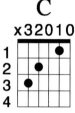

C7
x32410
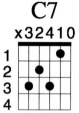

D
xx0132
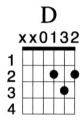

Dmin
xx0231
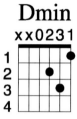

D7
xx0213
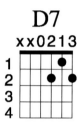

E
023100
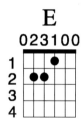

Em
023000
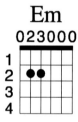

E7
020100
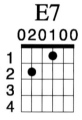

F
xx3211
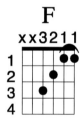

G
210003
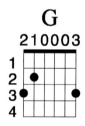

G7
320001
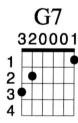

BARRE CHORDS

E-type
134211
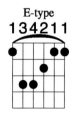

Emin-type
123111

E7-type
121211
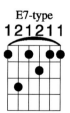

A-type
x12341
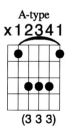
(3 3 3)

Amin-type
x13421
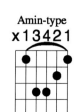

A7 type
x13121
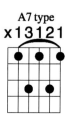

AUTHENTIC
BONGO RHY...MS

by BOB EVANS

TABLE OF CONTENTS

Cover photo supplied courtesy of Latin Percussion, Inc.

BIOGRAPHICAL NOTES

Bob Evans became interested in and began drumming at an early age through his father, who played drums. Drumming locally until induction into the Army he then spent 3 years in Special Service playing in marching bands and the post organized dance orchestras.

After service he enrolled in the Katherine Dunham School to study ethnic dancing and there was exposed to primitive drumming, at which he decided to give all his time and interest. At the Dunham school he studied authentic tribal and folk rhythms from two of Haiti's finest drummers, Papa Augustine and Narcisse.

After a tenure of playing Haitian songs and dances and the assimilation of Cuban rhythms he was soon featured as drum soloist in a number for an all Latin-American revue at the Boston Latin Quarter. This number was eventually placed in a long running show at the New York Latin Quarter.

Having worked primarily with dancers he became associated with dancer-choreographer, Peter Gennaro. As Mr. Gennaro's solo accompanist he played for 6 years for his numerous night club and television appearances plus his classes in Jazz.

Mr. Evans was the rehearsal drummer for the Duke Ellington television show, "A Drum Is A Woman", composing all the solo conga drum sequences.

He has appeared in the following musicals in New York: "Guys & Dolls", "The Pajama Game", "Damn Yankees", and "The Music Man". In addition to theatre appearances he has also recorded with many of the famous Latin orchestras.

Mr. Evans today is considered to be one of the foremost percussion authorities on Latin-American rhythms and music, and his knowledge and understanding are very well demonstrated in this book.

HAB14

DEFINITION OF MUSICAL TERMS AND SIGNS

The five parallel and equi-distant lines represent the staff.

The "F" clef is the clef that drum music is written in. The Bongos are written in the "G" clef when used in score form with other drums.

The time signature establishes the meter which designates the number of beats to a measure and the note value that receives one beat.

The bar line, drawn vertically across the staff marks off the measures which are determined by the time signature.

A double bar is placed at the end of a composition or before a change of time signature.

A brace is a line connecting two or more staffs, and it signifies that parts are to be played simultaneously.

The notes in the upper space are for the drum. The lower notes are beats for the foot and will help clarify the note values of the drum line.

These signs are repeat marks which means the section placed between them is to be repeated again.

The simile means the measure is played exactly the same as the previous measure.

Two measures are to be played exactly the same as the previous two measures.

A wedge placed over a note designates a sharp accent.

The tie, placed between two notes means when the first note is played it is carried over through the time value of the second note.

These are volume marks. The first one, CRESCENDO, represents a gradual increase in volume to the loudest point and the second, DECRESCENDO, represents a gradual decrease in volume from the loudest point to its softest.

HAB14

NOTATION OF TIME VALUES

Notes, dots and rests are the means of representing time values. The note values are:

𝅝 – Whole note   ♪ – Eighth note

𝅗𝅥 – Half note   𝅘𝅥𝅯 – Sixteenth note

♩ – Quarter note   𝅘𝅥𝅰 – Thirty-second note

The following symbols represent the corresponding rest values:

▬ – Whole rest   𝄾 – Eighth rest

▬ – Half rest   𝄿 – Sixteenth rest

𝄽 – Quarter rest   𝅀 – Thirty-second rest

A dot placed after a note is equal to half the value of the note after which it is placed:

𝅝. – Whole note and half dot (𝅝 𝅗𝅥)

𝅗𝅥. – Half note and quarter dot (𝅗𝅥 ♩)

♩. – Quarter note and eighth dot (♩ ♪)

♪. – Eighth note and sixteenth dot (♪ 𝅘𝅥𝅯)

Dots may be used after rests to increase their time values. The dotted rest values are the same as the dotted note values.

TIME SIGNATURES

𝄴 is the musical symbol for 4/4 time.

𝄵 is the musical symbol for 2/2 time.

Common Time

When the upper number of the time signature is written in 2, 3, or 4, it is called common time:

$$\frac{2}{4}, \quad \frac{4}{2}, \quad \frac{2}{4}, \quad \frac{3}{4}, \quad \frac{2}{8}, \quad \frac{3}{8}, \quad \text{and} \quad \frac{4}{8}.$$

Compound Time

When the upper number of the time signature is written in 6, 9, or 12, it is called compound time and the accents divide the beats into threes or triplets:

$$\frac{6}{2}, \quad \frac{6}{4}, \quad \frac{9}{4}, \quad \frac{12}{4}, \quad \frac{6}{8}, \quad \frac{9}{8}, \quad \frac{12}{8}, \quad \text{and} \quad \frac{12}{16}.$$

TUMBAO

The word Tumbao means the bass beats upon which other more complex rhythmic patterns are built. They provide the basic rhythm for other drums that take a secondary counter-rhythm. This bass beat is usually retained as a repetitious pattern throughout set rhythms and also improvisations.

THE CINQUILLO

The most important single rhythm in Latin-American music, the common denominator that binds the majority of them together is a group of five notes that have been evolved and known as a Cinquillo.

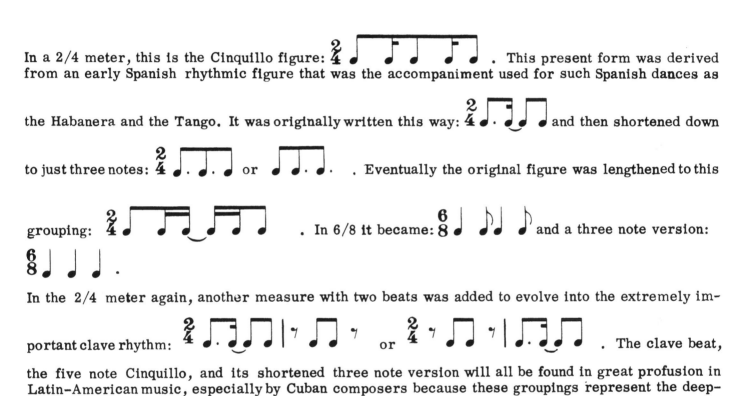

In a 2/4 meter, this is the Cinquillo figure: . This present form was derived from an early Spanish rhythmic figure that was the accompaniment used for such Spanish dances as the Habanera and the Tango. It was originally written this way: and then shortened down to just three notes: or . Eventually the original figure was lengthened to this grouping: . In 6/8 it became: and a three note version: .

In the 2/4 meter again, another measure with two beats was added to evolve into the extremely important clave rhythm: or . The clave beat, the five note Cinquillo, and its shortened three note version will all be found in great profusion in Latin-American music, especially by Cuban composers because these groupings represent the deepest emotional expressions that are to be found in Cuban music.

THE BONGO DRUM

Because of the physical differences between the Conga drum and the Bongos, the technique for each is quite different. The Bongos are smaller drums with a higher pitch which permits very fast playing. The two heads allow for a very definite tonal difference because the one head is larger than the other. The two heads are theoretically tuned a fifth apart, notes C to G for instance, but actually this isn't necessarily so because of the effect of the weather upon the heads and the necessary tension needed in each head to produce a resonant sound. Tunable heads with tensioning rods are the most practical since they can be pitched higher and lower according to tonal preference or tighter and looser according to the degree of humidity. These heads are not as resonant as the large Conga drum but they produce a dryer, intense sound which is more penetrating, and ideal for accenting rhythms.

HAB14

The Basic Latin-American Beat for Bongos

Known as the Martillo, this is the most commonly used beat for Bongos, and it should be mastered completely. The Martillo is effective for all rhythms from slow Boleros to fast Rumbas. It involves eight finger positions to complete one measure or pattern. Each stroke is explained and illustrated separately below:

Figure 1 – with the L. thumb pressing firmly strike the small head near the edge with the R. index finger.

Figure 2 – hit the small head with the last 3 fingers of the L. hand, lifting off the thumb and at the same time remove the R. index finger from the head.

Figure 3 – with the 3 fingers of the L. hand still remaining on the head, strike the small head near the edge with the R. middle finger.

Figure 4 – hit the small head with the L. thumb, lifting off the last 3 fingers and removing the R. middle finger.

Figure 5 – same as Figure 1.

Figure 6 – same as Figure 2.

Figure 7 – with the 3 fingers of the L. hand remaining on the small head, strike the large head near the edge with the R. middle finger.

Figure 8 – same as Figure 4.

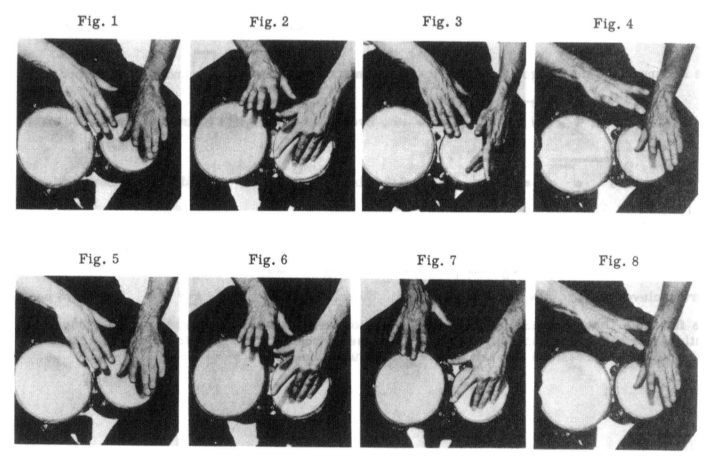

The movement of the left hand is achieved by using the extended index finger as a pivot and rocking the thumb and remaining three fingers around it. The fingering must be absolutely even as any anticipation or delay between the fingers in striking the head will throw the Martillo off completely.

In a 2/4 meter the strokes would fit in metrically as 16th notes, four to a quarter note. The Martillo is written out below with the picture numbers placed above the notes. The correct accenting is also added but remember, start slowly for even stroking and gradually increase your tempo for speed and endurance:

Stroking

In general, playing the whole hand is rarely used except in the solo or for effects. This drum is struck with the fingers. The two index fingers are the ones used, hitting the smaller head not in the middle but as near the edge on each side as is possible which gives the best sound as shown in FIGURE I:

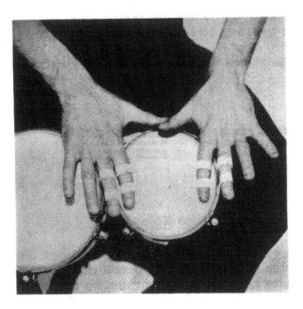

As you can see by the picture, the smaller head is to the player's left and the larger head on his right. The drum is held as shown, between the knees with the shell of the drum resting upon the calves of the legs. The position is reversed for left handed players.

Practice hitting the small drum with the index fingers in the proper position near the edge until you have clean, clear sounds. Hit the head with equal strength so that one hand won't be producing louder sounds than the other hand.

The larger head is not hit on opposite sides as is the smaller head but the two index fingers strike the head at the edge close to one another, as in FIGURE 2:

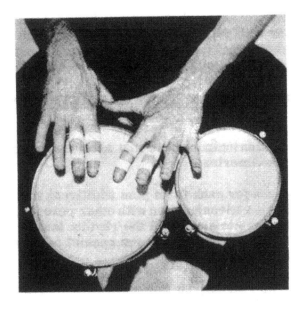

As is the case with the Conga drum, the fingers must snap off the head immediately after striking it or else the sound will be muffled and the percussive effect lost completely.

HAB14

Notation

In order to differentiate between the small bongo head and the large one, the notation will occur on different spaces in the staff. The large head will be written on the third space from the bottom while the notes for the small head will be written a space higher, or the fourth space from the bottom which makes reading for the two heads very easy. The notes on the first space are foot beats in order to clarify the bongo rhythms. The Bongo drum is written in the bass clef except when it is to be played simultaneously with a Conga drum. Then the Bongo drum part is written on the treble clef's leger lines and the Conga drum on the bass clef below them.

The following example shows the space notation for both Bongo heads:

Small Bongo head →
Large Bongo head →
Foot beats →

Grace Notes

In the drum family the relation of the Bongos to the other larger drums is one of accents and embellishments. Because of the smallness of the heads this drum allows for a great velocity in the beats and rhythms used. Dexterity and fast stroking must be part of the playing technique. Grace notes are used constantly as they themselves are embellishment figures requiring clean stroking.

Grace notes receive no musical value and are written before the meter note as a smaller note. The Flam is written this way: and is executed with a slight time lapse between the two notes----------------almost simultaneously.

The Three Stroke is written this way: with the accent occuring on the metered note. The Grace notes are usually executed much lighter than is the main note to which they are attached.

The Four Stroke is usually written as a triplet before the metered note this way: . In executing the Four Stroke the same dynamics apply as in the Flam and the Three Stroke. Longer grace note strokes usually take up so much metered time that they are written as notes of value within the measure or measures.

As the Bongo is mostly a counter-rhythm drum for accenting and embellishing, many of the written rhythms will sound better with the support of a Conga drum to supply a basic tumbao beat. The Bongo may use Congo drum rhythms if they are to be played alone which will provide them with more basic, stronger beats. Bongo and Conga drum rhythms are often interchangeable.

AUTHENTIC LATIN-AMERICAN RHYTHMS FOR THE BONGO DRUM

The rhythms in this section include those that are the most popular in the United States and the most representative of Latin-America.

The basic rhythm is given for each form plus additional variations. Some of the variations are to be used as tumbaos and also in conjunction with other percussion instruments while some variations are full enough in themselves to supply all the rhythm that is necessary. The amount of percussion needed and also what is available to you plus the special demands of a particular arrangement will determine which type of variation to use.

It is to be understood that throughout this section all repeat marks around the patterns and variations are to be interpreted as being a continuous repeat, that is, a one, two, or four measure phrase is to be repeated as long as it is desirable to do so. A one measure pattern could supply the rhythm throughout a whole number or be played only once.

On the first three rhythms shown hand drums are not played at all, but because these rhythms are so important in Latin-American music the basic rhythm of each is shown in order to become familiar with them and to show their characteristic differences from the other rhythms.

In each rhythm, one example is chosen and scored with a Bongo drum part in order to show its practical use when combined with another rhythm. The choice of the two rhythms that are put together in each case is purely arbitrary since there are usually many other rhythmic possibilities that could have been used.

The Bongo drum parts will be written on the treble clef staff and the Conga drum parts in the bass clef below.

JOROPO

The Joropo is the most characteristic rhythm of Venezuela. It's in a quick tempo in either 6/8 or 3/4 with short melodic phrases and a strongly accented but simple and steady accompaniment. "Ay Trigueña" is a Joropo. A similar rhythm is the Pasillo from Colombia.

The basic rhythm is $\frac{3}{4}$ ♪♪♪ or ♪♪ ♪♪ which is played on a snare drum with the accent on the first beat of the measure as a roll.

PASO DOBLE

Paso Doble, meaning "double step" is a fast march in which hand drums are not used. The American Paso Doble, becoming popular in 1926 is in 3/4 meter and the Spanish Paso Doble is in 2/4. "Lady Of Spain" is an American Paso Doble and "Espana Cañi" is a Spanish Paso Doble.

Usually played on a snare drum the basic rhythms of both are in a two bar phrase. The American: $\frac{3}{4}$ ♪♪♪♪♪ | ♪♪♪ . The Spanish: $\frac{2}{4}$ ♪♪♪♪ | ♪♪ .

TANGO

Originated by the Moorish gypsies who called it the Milonga, the Tango was brought to Spain by them and eventually to Cuba by Negro slaves. Out of the slums of Buenos Aires it was refined and brought to the U. S. in 1914.

The Tango and the Habanera are practically identical, both having the same rhythmic figure: ♪♪♪♪ . The two most important forms of Tango are the Spanish and the Argentine although there is a Brazilian Tango which is much more languid and sentimental. The Spanish Tango is in 2/4 and the Argentine Tango in 4/4 with the accent on the "and" count of four. The popular song, "It Takes Two To Tango" is in a Spanish Tango rhythm and "La Cumparsita" is in the Argentine. No hand drums are played in either Tango.

The basic Spanish Tango rhythm is: $\frac{4}{8}$ ♪♪♪♪ which is played in two bar phrases on a snare drum this way: $\frac{4}{8}$ ♪♪♪♪♪ | ♪♪♪♪ . The basic Argentine Tango rhythm is: $\frac{4}{4}$ ♪♪♪♪ . It would be played on a snare drum in two bar phrases with a press roll on the "and" count of four, as these two examples show:

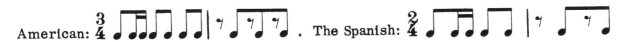

BEGUINE

Named after the French word "bégin", meaning flirtation, the Beguine originated on the Isles of St. Lucia and Martinique.

Hand drums are used with Beguines but just to tastefully maintain the flavor. The most popular Beguine would be "Begin The Beguine".

In the basic rhythm the accent's on the "and" count of one:

The basic rhythm accents the "and" count of one.

The Bongo drum will play an unaccented rhythm against this basic beat to serve as a background support:

Another two measure phrase with accents on the last half of the second measure:

This last rhythm stays strictly in the Beguine's rhythmic pattern and has a nice flow and continuity:

R — RIGHT HAND
L — LEFT HAND

The first example above is chosen to be shown with a Conga drum part. The basic accent is retained in the Conga drum rhythm:

SAMBA

This is the national dance of Brazil and although derived from the Maxixe, it has its origin in African rhythms. A violent and fast rural type with great syncopation exists but a refined city version came to New York in 1929.

The three characteristics of the Samba are a fast tempo, 2/4 meter, and a major key. "Tico Tico" and "Brazil", which is a Samba-Cançao, are good examples of popular Samba.

Originally played on a tambourine this is the basic rhythm in a two bar phrase:

The Bongo reiterates the basic Samba rhythm with this pattern of even notes:

A more syncopated two measure pattern with basic accents:

Another variation which retains basic accents:

The first beat of the measure is taken on the smaller Bongo head for this variation:

A two measure pattern for a fast Samba, adding accents before and after the basic second beat accent:

The following is example 3 with the basic Conga drum pattern as the tumbao:

HAB14

12

BAION

Another popular rhythm from Brazil is the Baion, a similar form to the Samba, and at times it is so alike that it's difficult to identify it as a Baion. The difference between the two is in the rhythmic pulse and general feeling. In the Baion the rhythm is more staccato while the melodic line is smoother and even flowing. In the Samba often the staccato feeling is in the melodic line while the rhythm has more of a rolling feeling. Like the Samba the Baion has its strong accent on the second beat of the measure. "Delicado" and "Anna" are Baions although other music may be played in this manner.

The basic rhythm of the Baion is the same as the basic Conga drum pattern:

The basic rhythm with the rolling 16th note figure added:

The same pattern as above only with a change of heads:

The 8th and 16th note figure changes the first measure:

In this rhythm the 8th and 16th note figure is a second measure rhythm now:

The Baion rhythm defined by accents in the following all 16th note example:

The basic rhythm goes to the Conga drum part to support the above example 5:

GUAJIRA

The rural Guajira takes its name from the Guajiros, peasants of the interior of Cuba. Related to the Punto, in its pure form it is written by alternating meters. Usually there is an eight measure intro in 6/8 meter and then the main body is either one measure of 3/4 and one measure of 6/8 or else it's a measure of 3/4 alternating with two measures of 3/8. With the two measures of 3/8 it has been called a Zarandillo, a form of Guajira. A later Guajira evolved in binary form. The first section is in 6/8 written in the minor and the second section is in 2/4, and written in the major. The last form, a city variety, is in 2/4 and resembles the Conga. This is the one using the most percussion and the one performed by orchestras.

Through all of these forms the Guajira has retained its identity by its melodic characteristics which are folksy, comparable to our "country and western" music.

The rhythm also combines well with other rhythms forming such hybrid forms as the Guajira-Son and the Guajira-Zapateo. "Junto Al Rio" and "Amor Carreteo" are typical Guajiras.

The following Guajira rhythms for the Bongo drum are the 2/4 variety. In this meter they are simple, fairly even beats. The tempo is usually Andantino Mosso.

The basic rhythm is the following from which the examples vary very little:

The simplicity of the form is carried on with this rhythm which is little more than the basic pattern:

Two 8th notes are added on the second quarter note:

Two more 8th notes are added and a shift of heads also:

Another head switch gives us this variation:

A slight embellishment by adding two 16th notes to the last quarter note:

Both heads on the Bongo drum are struck simultaneously on the first 16th note of the second quarter note. The Conga drum part states the basic rhythm as a support:

HAB14

CONGA

The Conga is the Rumba of the streets. Of Afro-Cuban origin this carnival and parade rhythm in march tempo was brought to the U. S. during the late 30's. As is true of the Rumba and the Calypso, besides drums, rhythm is often augmented by using kitchen utensils such as pots & pans, spoons, bottles, etc.

The Conga has left an indelible mark on Latin rhythms, having a distinguished strong accent on the "and" count of two in the second measure of a two measure phrase. Often this unique "push beat" will be found on the "and" count of two in the first measure instead of in the second measure.

"Para Vigo Me Voy", "Chambelona", and "Uno, Dos Y Tres" are true Congas although almost any music in 2/4 can be played with this distinctive beat.

The Conga has disappeared as a violent dance form but it has been absorbed and formalized into the Comparsa.

The basic Conga beat in 2/4 is:

The flam is added in front of every "push beat" for Bongo playing. Basic rhythm is again stated clearly in this example:

Rhythmic emphasis is changed with the strokes on the two and four of the first measure:

A galloping action is achieved by the added 8th notes:

Triplets in the first measure give us another variation:

Broken sets of triplets add further irregularity to the Conga pattern:

The last two triplet variations may be joined for a four measure phrase in this manner:

The broken sets of triplets of example 5 contrast well with the basic rhythm held in the Conga drum part:

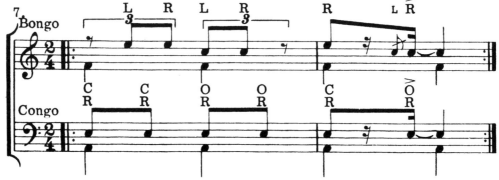

CALYPSO

A rhythm from Trinidad, the characteristic beat is of African origin. Although of a simple basic rhythm Calypso is quite a free form since not only is the rhythm improvised but also the melody and lyrics, often either or both being made up on the spot. The words are satirical about topical and current events. These polysyllabic words are often rephrased completely out of meter. Cinquillo rhythms are found all through Calypso accompaniments.

In 2/4 the accent occurs on the "and" count of two. The basic rhythm is:

This first one is a good repetitive pattern:

This two measure rhythm can be used to good advantage in a medium tempo:

The left hand accents on the small head provide a contrasting rhythm to the Conga drum:

A two measure phrase with the simple accent retained:

The dotted 16ths and the 32nd notes give a naturally accented rhythm without having to use signs to indicate them:

The two measure example 3 is supported by the rocking syncopation of this Conga rhythm:

HAB14

This rhythm was brought by African slaves into Cuba where it has remained unchanged except by embellishments. Unless composed specifically for a suite, Afro is not written because other slow Latin-American music in four such as the Bolero Rumba can be played in an Afro style. The basic rhythm is a one measure phrase with the distinguishing accents on "three and four". The basic rhythm:

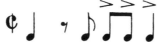

The basic Afro beat stated very simply:

Adding the two 16th notes to the first quarter gives us the most popularly used Afro rhythm for Bongo drum:

The above pattern is embellished by the addition of triplets to the first quarter note:

The same variation as above only with a tonal change:

A dotted 8th and a 16th syncopate the first quarter note:

The 16th note tripled rhythm of example 3 is played with a Conga drum rhythm containing quarter note triplets:

A great many primitive rituals and religious songs and dances are done in this 6/8 meter which accounts for its prevalence in Latin-American music, even when it is used in a 2/4 meter as a contrasting counter-rhythm, i. e., when the Conga drum is in 2/4 and the Bongo & Timbale in 6/8. Improvising in 6/8 is ideal because of the nice rhythmic pulse and easier to achieve continuity this meter affords.

Basic Afro 6/8 has the accents on the "one" and "four" of the six 8th notes in the measure. This is the pulse of the 6/8:

Establishing a simple rhythm like this first so that it can be used later as the basis for variations:

Another one measure phrase, repeated for a short time and then embellished upon:

A two measure rhythm quite complete in itself:

A rhythm almost the reverse of the example above:

A four measure phrase quite complete for continuous repetition:

The broken rhythmic pattern of example 5 can be used with a more even rhythm such as the complimentary Conga drum rhythm shown below:

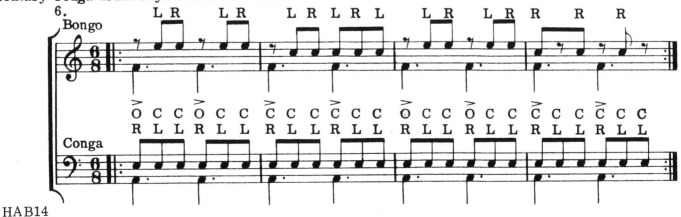

HAB14

NAÑIGO

Nañigo is taken from a ritualistic initiation dance in Africa, the Nañiga. It is an Afro 6/8 rhythm with a distinctive rhythmic beat. A dance done at festivals and carnivals in Cuba, it is sometimes played continuously for days.

Nañigo rhythm is distinguished by a two measure phrase usually done on a cowbell. The basic Nañigo is: 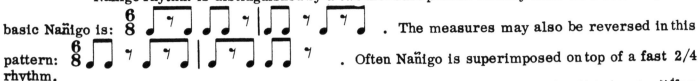 . The measures may also be reversed in this pattern:  . Often Nañigo is superimposed on top of a fast 2/4 rhythm.

The Bongos strengthen the beat by taking the first part of the rhythm and repeating it twice on different heads:

A two measure pattern with the 8th notes giving the effect of quarter note triplets in the second measure:

These two rhythms can be put together for an excellent four measure phrase:

The same pattern as the second example above only this time in the second measure the quarter note triplet figure starts on the second 8th note instead of the first. Using the second example first these two rhythms can also be used together to form a four measure phrase:

The basic Nanigo rhythm as stroked on the Bongo:

An embellishing rhythm to be used when the basic rhythm is strongly stated by other percussion instruments:

The four measure broken pattern of example 4 stands out in relief against the basic Nañigo beat held down by the Conga drum part:

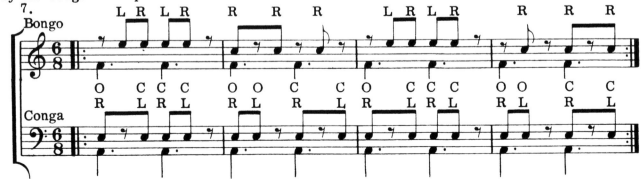

GUARACHA

The Guaracha presents a problem in trying to classify it because it has been written in so many different meters. Some have been written in 2/4, some in 3/4, and others in 6/8. Sung with guitar accompaniment the 6/8 meter has been alternated every other measure with either 3/4 or 2/4. Besides those possibilities, the melody may be anywhere from two to twelve measures in length which is repeated throughout.

The most popular form is the fast 2/4 variety which is played by dance orchestras. The Mexican Sequidilla and Jaleo are similar in this form. "La Burrita Enamorada" and "La Palmira" are in the folk forms while the popular "La Cumbanchero" is a fast 2/4 Guaracha. It has been combined with other rhythms to form hybrids such as the Guaracha-Mambo, Guaracha-Prégon, and Guaracha-Rumba. Shortened versions of the Cinquillo will be found in Guaracha accompaniments.

In the basic rhythm the beats are fairly even with the accented pulse on the last two 16th notes of the second beat:

All these rhythms are usually played very fast. This one in particular can be stroked at very fast tempos:

The first pattern syncopated by leaving out the stroke on the second quarter note:

Full stroking with accents added for correct rhythmic stress:

The same stroking but different accents and different heads give the rhythm a different character from the rest:

A two measure pattern for more drive and continuity:

For a complete driving beat this all accented rhythm at a fast tempo is effective:

The driving rhythm of example 6 is shown with the basic rhythm as played by the Conga drum:

HAB14

RUMBA

The Rumba, with its roots in Africa can be traced by historical accounts as it spread from Iberia all through the West Indies and then to Cuba. That is why so many rhythms are Rumba-type such as the Calypso, Guaracha, and the Sons. Like the Guaracha it usually is taken at a very fast tempo, (but not necessarily).

Finally arriving in the U. S. in 1929, well watered down, it became an extremely popular dance form. In a 2/4 meter the characteristic Rumba beat is the Cinquillo figure taken by the claves for a two measure phrase:
More than any other rhythm the clave beat is the most representative of a Rumba. Against this work counter-rhythms of which the simplest is a basic figure common also to Calypso:
"Siboney" and "The Peanut Vendor" are Rumbas that are very often played very fast.
A two measure pattern to be used at a fast tempo:

The added accents in the second measure give the same pattern more drive:

A little more difficult but an interesting Rumba variation:

Another rhythm by adding a tonal change and an increase in accents:

These short figures in the first measure will give variety to and break up the 16th note pattern characteristic of these fast 2/4 Bongo variations:

A little more rhythmic variety by breaking up the second measure into accented 8th note triplets:

The drive of example 2 is helped along by the pattern the Conga drum uses:

CUBAN BOLERO

The Cuban Bolero is in 2/4 meter and of moderate to slow tempo. An 8th and two 16th notes on the first quarter beat identifies the Cuban Bolero figure which was adapted from the triplet figure of the classical Spanish Bolero which is in 3/4.

The basic rhythm of the Cuban Bolero is:  or the Cinquillo figure

which is written this way:  . The importance of the Bolero form is its use in combination with other Latin-American rhythms, such as the Bolero-Son, Bolero-Cançion, and the Bolero-Rumba.

Examples of Bolero for the Bongo drum will be shown in a Bolero-Rumba rhythm since the 8th and two 16th note figure and Bolero flavor are retained in this combined form.

"Por Que Dudas" and "Las Perlas de tu Boca" are true Cuban Boleros.

BOLERO-RUMBA

The Rumba has now been relieved of its fast, driving pace, its strong accents, and its obliquely syncopated rhythms by merging with Bolero rhythms. The tempo is moderate, the meter is in a four, and although the triplet figure isn't as evident as it is in the straight Bolero, it is still suggested throughout. The pulse, dance, and feeling is still Rumba but now slower and with more elegance. "Besame Mucho" and "Siboney" are Bolero-Rumbas.

The basic rhythm is distinguishable by an 8th and two 16th notes on the first quarter:

The basic rhythm broken up tonally:

The same figure is repeated twice in the same measure by using the example above as a first measure pattern. A second measure of the basic rhythm is added:

When there is sufficient emphasis on the downbeat from the other instruments this variation that starts on the second half of the first beat with a Bolero triplet figure is a good one to use:

This is not as syncopated as the last rhythm but it has the down beat preceding the triplet figure:

HAB14

The triplet figure is split between heads. Try to execute the change of heads as evenly as possible so as not to distort the timing of the triplet and 8th note that follows:

This is a good break to use as the fourth or the eighth measure at the end of a musical phrase. Don't rush the 8th note triplets. Give each one its full value:

Both examples 5 and 6 are shown with a Conga drum part. The 8th note triplets stand out as a counter-rhythm against the basic rhythm as stroked by the Conga drum:

SPANISH BOLERO

The classical Spanish Bolero is not of folk origin, having been invented by a dancer in 1780. Also known under the names of Gachcha and Giatana, it is in 3/4 and usually written in the minor key in a moderate to very slow tempo.

The Cuban Bolero in 2/4 was originally derived from the Spanish Bolero and both are practically identical in tempo, mood, and feeling. Only the difference in meter and the purposes for which they are used distinguishes one from the other, as in the combining of the Cuban Bolero with the Rumba.

The characteristic figure of a Spanish Bolero is a triplet which is predominant in the music. The figure is evident in all of the following examples except for the first one:

MERENGUÉ

Of Spanish-Negro origin the Merengué is the national dance of the Dominican Republic, a sister island of Haiti. Possibly derived from an African dance, the Meringha, in rhythm it is very similar to the Punto.

The Spanish Merengué is usually written in the major key while the Haitian Meringué (different spelling) is usually in the minor and is sung in French.

In binary form, the first theme is 16 measures, two periods of equal length and the second theme also of 16 measures. In a moderate 2/4 meter the rhythmic pattern is a two measure phrase. The characteristic accents occur on four 16th notes on the second beat in the second measure. The accents are sometimes put in the first measure and carried over to the down beat of the next measure, but it isn't used as often as the accented second measure way is. "Mi Carino" and "La Empaliza" are good Merengués. Other 2/4 music may be adapted to the Merengué style.

This is the basic Merengué rhythm:

This is the basic rhythm reversed with the accents in the first measure now:

The first example in each case will be the Merengué pattern with the accents on the four 16th notes that occur on the second beat of the second measure, and the example to the right of it will be the reverse of that pattern with the accents occuring on the second beat of the first measure. Both forms are used.

The first is the basic Merengué rhythm as stated on the Bongos:

A slight variation by placing the 16th note on the smaller head:

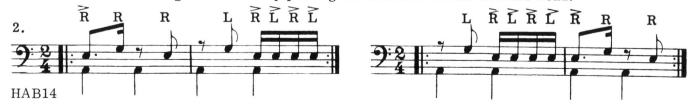

HAB14

A strong accent on the first downbeat from the other instruments allows this pattern of a quarter rest:

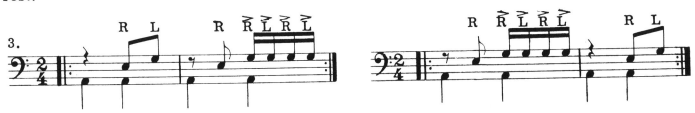

The same pattern as above with an 8th and a 16th note figure added:

Without any unnecessary embellishments this is about as busy as a Merengué rhythm for one instrument should be. The use of both heads gives the rhythm a nice bounce:

Essentially the same pattern as the one above less an 8th note and plus a 16th note:

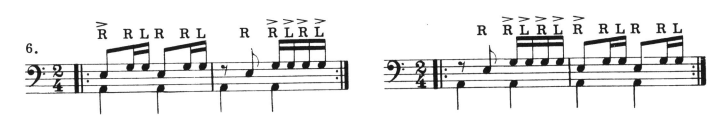

The syncopated beat of example 2 is aided by the forward drive of the accented downbeats and 16th notes in the Conga drum line:

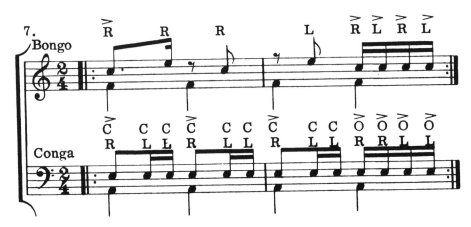

MAMBO

The most recent contribution to United States' dance fads from Latin-America is the Mambo. In a way this is as much an American product as it is Latin because although the rhythms and dance movements are Cuban, the melodies and especially the harmonies are the creations of the American Negro. Mambo is the merger of Cuban rhythms and modern contemporary jazz harmonies.

The form is not a folk form but an amalgamation of many sophisticated elements. The rhythm is derived from Rumba but with much stronger accenting, in present day interpretations. Rhythm almost dominates the melodies and is so persuasive that it has been used, unfortunately, on material that is both inferior and/or inappropriate to this rhythm, which has only succeeded in weakening the form.

Almost any music in a four may be played as a Mambo, but an excellently written and recorded example is Prez Prado's Mambo #5.

Taken from the Rumba, the basic rhythm has retained the accented "four and" 8th notes on the last beat of the measure, and to this has been added a very strongly accented quarter note on

the second beat of the measure. The following is the Mambo basic rhythm:
The Mambo can be played from very fast to moderately slow. The fast or single Mambo has the four feeling of the Bolero and Cha Cha.

Examples will be shown first of the single Mambo and then those for double Mambo. Most of these rhythms can be interchanged of course because there is no set boundary so to speak between the single and double Mambo, the terms themselves often arbitrary, for the convenience of identification.

SINGLE MAMBO

This first figure, more of an embellishment requiring other percussive support, is very intense and shouldn't be repeated for too long since it isn't a rhythm for sustaining and maintaining a driving beat. At a fast tempo eight measures would be sufficient:

At a fast tempo this figure is a driving beat:

In the single Mambo a phrase usually takes two measures to complete. This pattern is a good two measure fast phrase:

The dotted 8th and the 16th give this rhythm a swinging beat. It's a good figure to use in back of an instrumental soloist:

HAB14

A similar rhythm to the example above which has been extended to a two measure phrase:

Another fast tempo pattern using a drive in the first measure on the lower drum:

A fast Mambo beat that pushes the rhythm ahead. Observe all accents for this drive:

Example 2 is meant to move along at a fast tempo. A Conga drum pattern which is easy to execute at these fast tempos is shown with it:

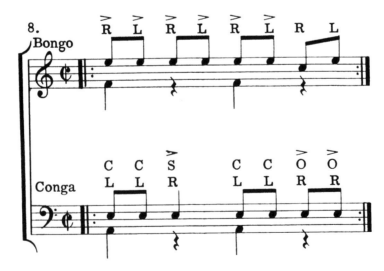

DOUBLE MAMBO

In this one measure rhythm both heads are hit simultaneously with the left and right forefingers on the fourth beat of the measure:

In the next rhythm observe that in the syncopation on the first two beats of the measure the first quarter note has an 8th rest and the second quarter has a 16th rest. This is obviously used with other percussion instruments since the downbeat is not stated:

The same need for rhythmic support also holds true for this one measure counter-rhythm:

The right hand remains on the large head while the left alternates between the small and the large:

A rhythm played mostly by the left hand. In the first measure the stroking could be done alternating hands, but the dynamic effect comes out much smoother using one hand:

Again even dynamics are achieved by not alternating hands on the small head. In the second measure it makes the triplet figures stand out more and the accented left hand gives an irregular rhythmic effect. Use all accent markings:

Example 6 above is used with its 8th note triplet figures in the last half of the second measure. The Conga drum part has quarter note triplets in the first half of its second measure which makes them fit in well with one another:

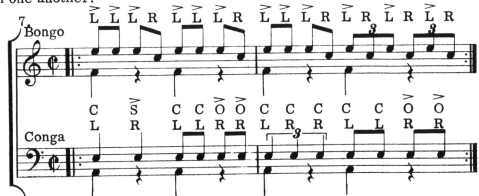

HAB14

The most recent hybrid form to evolve from the influences of the Bolero-Rumba, Double Mambo, and Jazz is the Cha Cha. In the Cha Cha the rhythmic pulse is in a very definite four, that is, that each quarter note in the measure is strongly but evenly accented. The basic rhythm for the Conga drum is still an open tone "four and" 8th note figure on the last quarter beat of the measure. As is the case with non-folk forms, any music in four can be played as a Cha Cha, but the music written

putting the Cha Cha Cha (𝅘𝅥 𝅘𝅥 𝅗𝅥.) on the first two beats of the measure gives the right emphasis and feeling for the dancers who can choose to Cha Cha with the figure or against it.

The basic Conga drum rhythm is: 𝄴 𝅘𝅥 𝅘𝅥 𝅘𝅥 𝅘𝅥𝅘𝅥

The two one measure examples below are easy counter-rhythms to be used with Conga drum support:

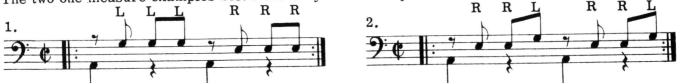

A nice rhythm that can be used at any tempo:

Another embellishing rhythm that will need Conga drum support because of the 8th note rests on the downbeats:

This rhythm is the most effective at slow tempos where each beat is definite and deliberate:

An almost identical two measures except for the 16th notes in the second measure:

A syncopated two measures with the left hand on the small head stating all the weaker beats of this rhythm:

The broken rhythm of example 7 is used with the more even rhythm and basic accents of the accompanying Conga drum part:

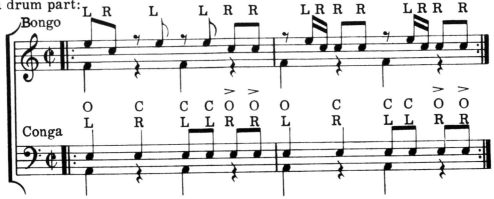

SON

The Son is a Cuban development of a Spanish type folk song that came to Havana in 1916, replacing the Danzon in popularity. In a 2/4 meter it is sung in chorus with a contrasting motive for solo voice. It is made up of two sections, the first being an original refrain of not more than 8 measures and the second section, the stronger of the two being a rhythmic refrain of not more than 4 measures that are repeated over and over again, called a Montuno. Melodically simple but highly syncopated its rhythmic structure is based on a Cinquillo () in which the last 8th note is split into 16ths as in the following example:

The five examples below are the most basic and characteristic rhythms used in Sons:

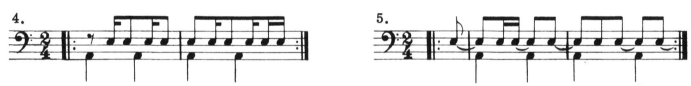

"Sun Sun Paloma" and "La Guayabera" are pure Sons but because of the simplicity and adaptability of its melodic lines and its highly syncopated rhythms the Son has been more universally used when it is combined with other rhythms such as the Rumba, which it most resembles. Some of the hybrid forms resulting from these mergers are:

Rumba-Son - A complete synthesis of the melodies and rhythms of both.

Son-Afro Cubano - An extension of the Son with strong syncopation, it has African melodies and words. "Babalu" is a Son-Afro Cubano.

Bolero-Son - This time the rhythmic patterns come from the Bolero. Beginning in a slow tempo it speeds up halfway through to a Montuno.

Samba-Son - Rhythmically more aggressive and played with much abandon as a resurrection of its original vital form.

Son-Oriental - Less percussive and more melodically interesting since the melodies used are Spanish interpretations of oriental influences.

Tango-Son - The Spanish Habanera rhythm (♪♪♪♪) combines with the Son because this Tango figure is common to both forms. "Mama Ines" is a Tango-Son.

Son-Montuno - Because the Montuno is an intregal part of Son, they become an unseparable entity, one and the same thing. The Montuno, taken up next, will show the counter-rhythms and polymetrics of the Son as played in Montuno Sections.

HAB14

MONTUNO

Montuno is not a rhythm but a section of a dance or song form. It is the section of the music where the melody stops and the rhythm takes over. If there is a melodic figure it is generally a melo-rhythmic phrase of two but not more than four measures repeated indefinitely. This section is also used as rhythmic support for a solo instrument improvisation. Any Cuban rhythm can have a Motnuno section. Most of them do.

The Montuno may increase or double in tempo, change in meter, or both. Of indeterminate length, it is the one section where the drummers may take turns superimposing counter-rhythms and polymetrics upon improvised rhythmic figures.

The four and eight measure counter-rhythmic phrases below are to be used in soloing as figures repeated against ensemble rhythms. They may also be used tastefully as breaks and embellishments in the other melodic sections where the rhythmic patterns are more established. Excellent for soloing is the smallest drum of the Conga drum family, the Quinto. Actually, it's a highly polished, resonant box.

Repeat marks have been eliminated because these improvisations are meant to break away from the established rhythm and they would not usually be immediately repeated again.

While the Bongo is soloing during the Montuno section the heads are often struck with timbale sticks instead of the fingers in order to obtain a louder sound and sharper attack.

The first counter-rhythm for the Montuno section is a very fast 2/4. The first four measures show a figure which is used very often as an embellishment, both on Conga drum and Bongos. The last four measures has a 3/8 rhythm set into the 2/4 time signature:

The next pattern starts with a four stroke ruff followed by triplets. Don't rush the triplets. At a moderate tempo in four the triplets should have the feeling of being delayed to set up the sharp, staccato 16th notes on the small head. Observe the accents in the next two measures. Accent all the alternate head triplets in the last two measures. As you have no doubt noticed, this is a five measure phrase:

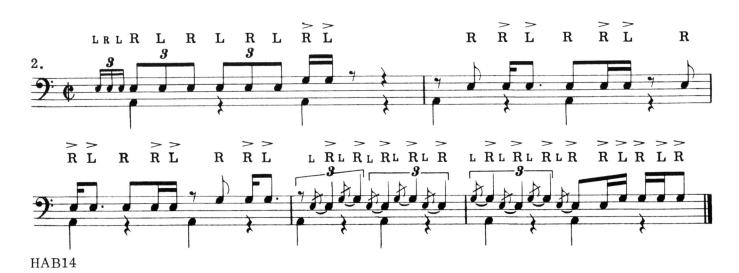

HAB14

A fast 2/4 tempo sets off this very familiar three note driving figure. The last four measures in triplets is predominately done with the right hand on the large head while the oddly accented off-beats are done by the left hand on the small head:

A twelve measure counter-rhythm in a fast 2/4 whereby the rhythmic pattern set in the first four measures diminishes by one 8th note in the next four measures, by two 16th notes in the next two measures, and by one more 8th note in the last two measures until just the accented left hand on the small head which has dominated the whole pattern remains:

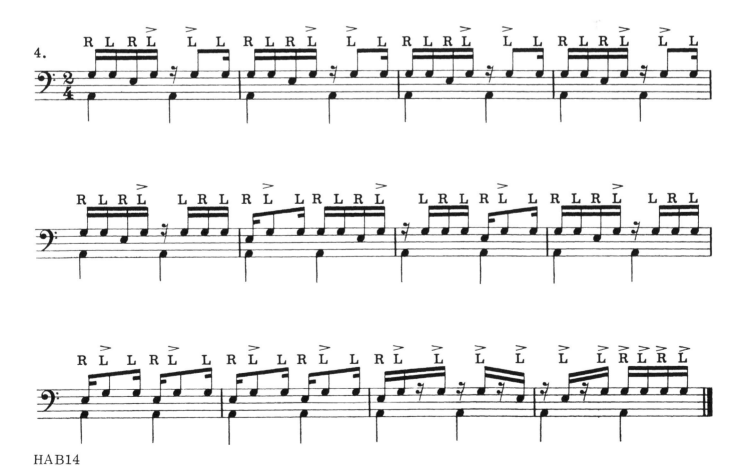

HAB14

32

The first two measures present another short rhythmic figure that is widely used on Bongo drums. It breaks into a metrically uneven pattern for the next two measures. The last four measures is a rhythm in 3/4 which pulses against the written 2/4 meter:

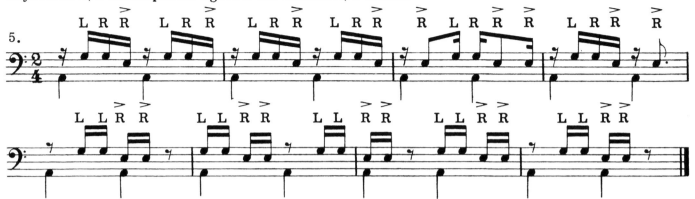

A very standard short percussive figure sets the pace in the first four measures of another 2/4 rhythm. The four pushing groups of notes help to set off the last four measures that repeat a short figure of a 16th rest, a 16th note, and two 8th notes, which, if it were put into its correct meter, would be 3/8:

The broken rhythmic patterns of example 5 are played against a simple Conga drum tumbao which must supply a rock-like foundation. The sets of three 16th notes in the first two measures are dependent upon this. The accented groups of two 16th note figures in the last four measures stand out in bold relief against the solid basic beat of the Conga drum:

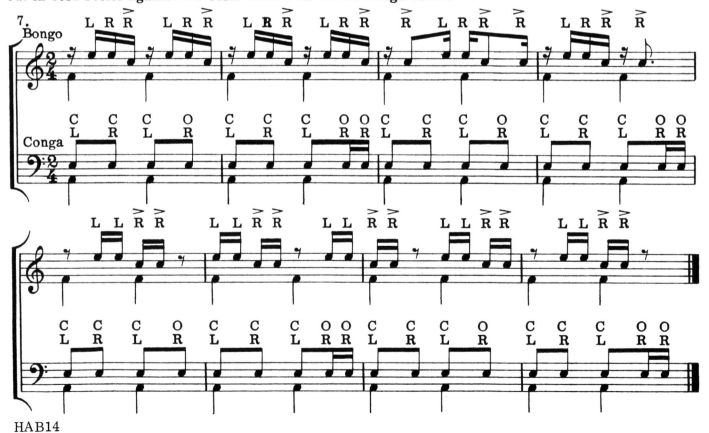